P9-BJD-756

## ADVANCE QUOTES FOR *DR. TOY'S SMART PLAY*

"*Dr. Toy's Smart Play* is a remarkable book. Although it is addressed to the parent (a child's first teacher) it will also contribute greatly to the teaching skills of teachers and child care workers. Dr. Auerbach includes an excellent overview of development beginning with infants through age twelve. Her resources are carefully chosen and well documented. As a longtime educator I strongly recommend this book. Play is a child's work and Dr. Toy details how a knowledge of and involvement in play can enhance a child's growth in all areas. I urge you to read this important, wonderful and insightful book."

Dr. Betty Halpern
Professor Emeritus
Sonoma State University

"Smart Play + Smart Parents = Smart Kids. Stevanne Auerbach, Ph.D., writes with the rare power of original analysis. *Smart Play* is the most significant, thorough and thoughtful book yet for parents wishing to match the right toy to the right stage of their child's early development. Follow Dr. Toy's prescription for a happy and skill-building childhood."

Richard D. Levy
Toy Inventor
Author, *Inside Santa's Workshop*

"Even before Friedrich Froebel 'invented' the kindergarten and popularized the slogan of 'Come, let us live with our children' during the 1840s, philosophers and wise parents recognized the importance of play. Developmental psychologists have emphasized its importance throughout the twentieth century. Recent scientific discoveries about physical changes in the brain when babies and young children are intellectually stimulated now validate this old idea. We recognize that school readiness begins at birth and that family members are the best possible Play Tutors. There are incredible opportunities but a lot of confusing alternatives. I'm delighted to know that *Dr. Toy's Smart Play* will be available to guide parents. It is filled with informed wisdom, inexpensive suggestions, and ideas for a lot of fun. Enjoy!"

Dorothy W. Hewes, Ph.D.
Professor Emeritus
Department of Child and Family Development
San Diego State University

"In *Dr. Toy's Smart Play*, Dr. Auerbach draws on her many years of experience as a teacher, child development specialist, parent educator, syndicated columnist, author of books, and of course parent and grandparent to bring together this inclusive, wise, clear book which provides excellent information based on her thorough understanding of both children and adults."

Edgar Klugman
Professor
Early Childhood Care and Education
Wheelock College, Boston

# DR. TOY'S SMART PLAY

## How to Raise a Child with a High PQ*

*Play Quotient

# DR. TOY'S SMART PLAY

## How to Raise a Child with a High PQ*

*Play Quotient*

### STEVANNE AUERBACH, PH.D./DR. TOY

St. Martin's Griffin
New York

DR. TOY'S SMART PLAY. Copyright © 1998 by Stevanne Auerbach, Ph.D. All rights reserved. Printed in the United States of America. No part of this book may be used or reproduced in any manner whatsoever without written permission except in the case of brief quotations embodied in critical articles or reviews. For information, address St. Martin's Press, 175 Fifth Avenue, New York, N.Y. 10010.

Design by Anne Scatto/PIXEL PRESS

Library of Congress Cataloging-in-Publication Data

Auerback, Stevanne.
Dr. Toy's smart play : how to raise a child with a high PQ / Stevanne Auerback.—1st ed.
p.      cm.
Includes bibliographical references.
ISBN 0-312-18089-6
1. Play—Psychological aspects. 2. Toys—Psychological aspects.
3. Child development.   I. Title.
BF717.A94      1998
649'.1—dc21

97-41485
CIP

First St. Martin's Griffin Edition: February 1998

10    9    8    7    6    5    4    3    2    1

# CONTENTS

# FOREWORD

In *Dr. Toy's Smart Play*, Dr. Auerbach draws on her many years of rich experience as a teacher, child development specialist, parent educator, syndicated columnist, author of books, and of course, as a parent and grandparent, to bring together this inclusive, wise, clearly written book. The information—which supports children's play at each stage of their development—also provides the essential background for understanding a child's current stage of life. Dr. Auerbach provides parents with the tools to interweave the joy of life, support their child's sense of self and self-worth, and guide and stimulate their own capacities to play and learn.

Play is <u>not automatic.</u> It is <u>learned</u>! The importance of play for children has been well-researched and demonstrated. For example, did you ever consider that play is one of the most important areas of activity in which children engage as they grow and develop? Did you know that play has been shown to contribute positively to a child's later education? Or that play is one of the most important factors in a child's learning how to interact with other children? Did you know that language development can be enhanced through children's play? And that abstract thinking, developed through play, forms a critical basis for a child's education, and exerts a strong influence into adult life?

I know that play is an art that many of us as adults may have forgotten. Our work-oriented society leaves very little room for renewal and re-creation. But imagine rediscovering your own childhood adventures, your favorite toy or game, and sharing these experiences with your own child. These are experiences which children may never forget. After all, they know you as parent, grandparent, aunt or uncle. Children may never have thought of you as having been a child who had favorite toys and play activities. The guidelines provided in this book can be helpful as you and your child undertake together a "play journey" which can enhance your relationship, your child's development, and your understanding of the processes of growth. Many joyful surprises await you. Have fun!

—Edgar Klugman
Professor
Early Childhood Care and Education
Wheelock College, Boston

# ACKNOWLEDGMENTS

Tracing my own pathways in play I gratefully acknowledge many individuals who assisted in shaping my rationale for thinking, writing, observing, and evaluating playthings. These people inspired, encouraged, and guided me toward completing this book. My experiences and interactions with them and with thousands of children and families over many years influenced my belief in the importance of play and playthings and belief that children's growth and learning is largely formed through their natural play patterns. In acknowledging I retrace some important steps in this long and dynamic process:

At Queens College in New York City, I was fortunate to have as my mentor the renowned educator Deborah Partridge Wolf, who showed me how to understand the child from all dimensions and to treat each one with respect as an individual. She also inspired me to write, think critically, and understand the relationships among play, learning, risking, experience, and environment. That treasured friendship has lasted throughout my life.

Later, teaching in S.W. Washington, D.C., I participated in an experimental new program of Theater Arts in Education with Arena Stage. I was inspired by working with Robert Alexander, a most astute, dedicated, playful person who taught actors, teachers, and students how techniques of improvisational play could move energy and improve learning. He and his colleague, Norman Gevanthor, provided me with rich training and experience.

My doctoral work brought me into contact with a pivotal professional leader, Glenn Nimnicht, who directed the Early Childhood Program at the Far West Laboratory for Educational Research and Development. Roy Fairfield, my Union Institute core faculty person, encouraged me to continue writing after completing my Ph.D. and to imagine writing as a playful process. His encouragement led to many books and articles and our friendship continues on-line.

Other writers, researchers, professionals, program directors, and colleagues inspired me along the way: Abraham Maslow, Barbara Biber, Bettye Caldwell, Brian Sutton Smith, Bruno Bettelheim, Catherine Garvey, Clare Cherry, Daniel Goleman, Debbie Wager, Diana Huss Green, Dorothy Hewes, Dotia Zovitkovsky, Edgar Klugman, Edward Elkin, Edward Zigler, Frank and Theresa Caplan, Fred Rogers, Howard Gardner, Ira J. Gordon, Jay Beckwith, Jean Piaget, Jerome Bruner, Jerome Kagan, Jim Prescott, Joanne Oppenheim, Judith Iaguzzi, Marguerite Kelly, Maria Montessori, Marion Wright Edelman, Marilyn Segal, Mary Sinker, Ron Lally, Routh Roufberg, Sandy Jones, Stella Resnick, Steven Kanor, Genevieve Landau, Joe Frost, Maria Piers, Robin Moore, T. Berry Brazelton, Vicki Lansky, Evelyn K. Oremland, and many others, who have been involved in expanding understanding of play.

I admire the great work that promotes play and learning by many professionals such as members of the National Association for the Education of Young Children, the International Association for the Child's Right to Play, Association for Childhood Education International, and those involved in service programs like toy lending libraries, Lekotek, child-life programs in hospitals, play therapy, play centers, preschool programs, parent cooperatives, Head Start, recreation centers, child-care centers, family day-care homes, Gymboree, Special Olympics, children's museums, children's libraries, Scouts, and UNICEF YMCA's and YWCA's and others. Thanks to all of you for your significant work on behalf of children as they discover and grow through direct experiences and extensions of play.

I appreciate those who belong to ASTRA (American Specialty Toy Retailing Association) and those who are members of the NSSEA (National School Supply and Equipment Association) and other groups that provide teachers and parents with tools that support learning. The owners of these stores strive for excellence in their selections and are of great service to their communities.

I was fortunate to be able to fulfill my dream to produce and direct the world's first toy museum devoted to the appreciation of the history of toys and where children could also play with new, developmentally sound toys of all kinds. The San Francisco International Toy Museum, a very special experience, was fulfilling for all participants and most of all for thousands of lucky children who were able to visit. I greatly appreciate the dedication over the years of the members of the Board of Directors and Advisory Committee, the community members who became involved, the many teachers, parents, and grandparents who came with children to play, and The Cannery, who offered to covert unused space into a special place for everyone to enjoy. For all of their dedication and heartfelt efforts I thank Frank Martin (we could not have made the toy museum happen without you), Henry Maggenti, Marilyn Borovoy, Mannie Luhn, Russ and Virginia Lowe, Mark and Nicholas Lowe, Deborah Gilden, Larry Paul, Andy Levison, Jean Bricker Mc-Clatchy, Clarence and Sara Woodard, Arlin Weinberger, Rebecca Kershner, Janet Crane, Andrea Laudate, Chris Martin, Senator Dianne Feinstein, Hasbro, Galoob, Dakin, LEGO Systems, Colorforms, many altruistic toy collectors, Dr. Winkie, the Morris Stulsaft Foundation, the Junior League, and Kohnke Printing for printing the *Toy Times* newspaper.

Over the twenty-five years I have been involved in the toy industry I have been fortunate to know many wonderful people who are committed to the well-being of children, including Tom Arbuckle, Ann Brown, Jean Carpenter, Bob Concannon, Brad Countryman, Alan Hassenfeld, Alan Hess, Karen Hewitt, Doug

Isaacson, William Killgallon, David LaFrennie, John Lee, Richard Levy, David Miller, Lane Nemeth, Harry Nizamian, Peter Reynolds, Frank Reysen, Jim Shea Jr., Scott Wisner, and Sy Ziv.

I am honored by all of the hundreds of large and small companies that have enthusiastically participated in the Dr. Toy's Best Products Program. They represent dedication to the child and the intention of providing the highest quality, innovative, developmental products to benefit children. I greatly respect those members of the TMA (Toy Manufacturers of America) and toy companies around the world dedicated to enhancing childhood with wholesome play and positive learning experiences.

A book is a collaborative effort. I am deeply appreciative of every person who assisted me along the way. I was very lucky to have Laurie Harper, of Sebastian Literary Agency in San Francisco, as my agent. She has always been there for me as a positive, insightful player. She had the foresight to bring my concept to one of the most enthusiastic, delightful, intelligent, and hard-working editors in the business, Heather Jackson at St. Martin's Press. She believed in the concept, knew why it was important, and became a champion for the book, responsive all the way. Thanks to her assistant Marc Resnick for being a great facilitator and Jill McFarlane for superb copyediting. I enthusiastically thank Kate Kelliher for her perfect side-by-side work on short deadlines. A fine editor and excellent writer, she is the kind of professional every author wants on his team.

I was fortunate to have a delightful, dedicated crew who helped me with the production of the manuscript from rough drafts to final copies, including multitalented Kazuko Nishita, who works diligently also on the Dr. Toy's Best Products Program; Winifred Stone, playful computer and gardening wiz; Jerry Kamstra, a friend and fellow writer who reviewed the manuscript and made many helpful comments; Janelle Berryman, Winifred Stone, and Ethan Campbell, who facilitated our process at critical junctures; Susan Gilchrist, for her laughter, excellent word processing, and research assistance; plus Ann Foley, for her fine word processing. Thanks to the staff at Krishna Copy Center, who always made sure copies were ready when needed, and William Branson, who helped make things move smoothly.

Gratitude to my superb editor at King Features Syndicate, Diane Eckert, who has been so perfect to work with on the Dr. Toy column. Recognition goes to all of the journalists and media people over these years who asked astute questions about play and playthings. Sharing my understanding on toys and play throughout the years motivated me to write more on this unlimited subject.

To my daughter, Amy Beth, and new grandson, Josiah, my heartfelt thanks for the inspiration to provide a primer on play to use for the whole of his growing up to assure the fullest of playtime joy. Thanks to my mother, Jeane R. Stockheim, for reading to me and inspiring cardboard and clothespin doll play and art and dance classes, and to my sister, Judith S. Schwartz, who shaped as if clay my most positive, earliest memories of play. To my cousin Marvin Ellin for believing in me, really being there after the earthquake and making a difference in my future.

Most of all my gratitude to my tech-savvy friend, life partner, and best playmate, Ralph Whitten, who truly understands how play expresses love.

*I dedicate this book to Ralph,*
*our children, grandchild,*
*and to all children,*
*may you always play in a safe, fun-filled world*

# INTRODUCTION

Do you recall what it was like to be a child at play, excited about discovery, eager to learn? First came shapes, colors, and sounds. Then there were toys. The toys a child plays with can unlock the door to learning, and each new experience helps to turn the key. How much did *we* learn through our play? How much can your child learn? You'll be surprised.

Take a moment and touch different objects around you—feel the textures: water, stucco, wood, plastic, glass, paper, fabric, skin, hair. . . . Most of us have forgotten the sheer joy of such discoveries!

Listen to sounds: laughter, talking, music, traffic, planes overhead, birds singing.

And the smells! Take in the aroma of food cooking with spices, sniff a bouquet of flowers, inhale the scent of newly cut grass or freshly baked bread.

Listen. Smell. Touch. See the things around you as a child sees them. Your child delights in each discovery from the simple to the complex. A baby absorbs information by reaching and touching, exploring the world with fingers and toes and mouth, and making contact with people and things.

If you observe your child playing you'll discover the learning processes he moves through at each stage of his development. If you are involved with these stages, you can experience the same magic your child is feeling.

As your little one grows, you provide toys to enhance her play. In this book I want to help you identify the product factors that will bring results and the right toy for the right stage of your youngster's progress. You will learn which kinds of toys sharpen observation and skills—and how to properly use these playthings so your child's thinking, feeling, self-expression, and physical dexterity are enhanced.

Our job as parents is to protect our children. I'll also point out characteristics of well-designed, sturdy, and safe products. You'll be acquainted with what to look for when selecting a toy, and you'll be provided with plenty of tips on how to introduce a toy to your child, how to gain his interest, and how to keep it.

You will find out how to balance *your* world with your child's play world and, most important of all, you'll learn to respect and understand the importance of play for children. You are your child's first "Big Toy." So the more you know about yourself, your child's development, and her play, the more you'll be able to use toys and yourself as learning and skill-building tools.

Although learning follows a sequence of gradual stages, each child learns at her own rate. Children cannot be pushed, pulled, rushed, or hurried. By absorbing, practicing, learning from mistakes, but most of all through discovery, each child will advance as his individuality dictates. This natural drive to discover through play becomes the essence of a happy childhood.

You will find out how to encourage your child's "PQ," his Play Quotient. As your child's Play Tutor, not only will you help your young one learn more, you'll also teach the skills to be happier and to get along better with others.

You can easily enhance your son or daughter's Play Quotient once you know how to choose toys carefully. And I think you'll enjoy playing as well. A playful parent encourages a child to be playful—a more playful child is a more aware, smarter, and more resilient one. The benefits to the whole family are enormous.

And do I need to mention how your whole relationship with your child will be strengthened?

Let's get you started as your child's Play Tutor.

Let's play!

# ONE

# The Importance of Play and Toys

Children love toys. From the colorful mobile overhead that attracts a baby's attention, to the tower of LEGO built by your little architect, well-designed toys stimulate your child's mind.

Young ones absorb messages from toys through all stages of their growth. The kinds of toys selected and how your youngster plays with them will influence how well she meets her learning potential. Choosing the right toys for her play is not easy. It can be a real challenge to find the right product, at the right time, for the right price.

And once you've done the above, there's the added challenge of getting the maximum value from the toy.

We've all heard about IQ (Intelligence Quotient). It is a classic predictor of your child's mental ability. I believe that your child's *PQ*, his *Play Quotient*, is an equally vital factor which affects how well your young one will attain the best of his physical, creative, and intellectual potentials.

Play is your child's work. Through play children practice the basic skills needed in the classroom—and in life. Guided play in the right environment will help your child gain the tools she needs to sharpen her thinking and heighten her sensitivity.

To assist your child in succeeding with skill-building, we will look at the different ways your child uses toys, and you'll become informed about finding the right toys, and skilled at helping your child expand his or her PQ.

## How Toys Work

Research conducted by child-development specialists points out that the first five years in the life of the child are of the greatest consequence. Many studies confirm the essential aspects of early mental, social, and neurological development. Some of the important researchers include Drs. Jerome Kagan (Harvard), Harry Chugani (Wayne State University), Janellen Huttenlocher (University of Chicago), Robert Modadi (UCLA), Jay Belsky (Penn State), and Patricia Kuhl (University of Washington). Corey Goodman and others at the University of California have linked genetic factors to learning and memory. Researchers at Baylor University found that children who do not play and are rarely touched have brains that are 20 to 30 percent smaller than normal for their age. Researchers at the University of Illinois found that toys stimulate 25 percent more brain synapses per neuron.

These early years are intensely formative: a period when children gain knowledge about themselves and about their environment, develop basic motor skills, discover many of their abilities, and gain the self-image and security that lasts a lifetime.

Like little sponges, children begin observing and absorbing from infancy. They learn by using all of their senses: sight, sound, smell, taste, and touch. Through observation, mimicry, and experimentation, children learn about the world around them and begin to gain mastery of essential skills.

When a parent is involved with a baby—smiling at her, creating silly and different sounds, making the baby laugh—the parent becomes the baby's first "Big Toy." Fathers who enjoy close contact with their infants soon are distinguished from the mother by the different ways they play. The baby quickly learns to respond to different persons' sounds and touches. Through such interchanges, the infant becomes conscious of individual people. Also, she becomes aware of the environment around her.

The secondary motor stage of child development occurs during these first five years. It is the time when the most rapid physical, emotional, and mental growth takes place. And at each stage of this development, a child needs different kinds of stimulation, enhanced by different kinds of toys and different play strategies.

# THE IMPORTANCE OF PLAY

## Play Principles

Play is a natural phenomenon. Before you examine the toys to be used by your young one, it helps if you understand the principles of play. Of particular importance is understanding that play enriches both sides of the brain—right and left hemispheres. Thus, the underlying principle of play, smart play, is that the child will gather essential experiences necessary for her fullest mental development.

As infants grow they play with innumerable things around them: their hands, their toes, sunbeams coming in through the window. At the same time they discover sounds; they babble and talk to themselves. They become conscious of the separate parts of their bodies; they make distinctions in color, light, and sound.

How children interact with people and elements in their environment is revealing. We should stand back and observe them. As we watch them play, we come to know their play process, the ways they get frustrated, their tolerance levels, and their curiosity and creative responses.

We want to be sure our children play with others of different ages and abilities so our own child can experience a full range of social interaction: patience, empathy, compassion, support, and honesty. The way he plays affects how he feels about himself.

A child plays alone, with other children, and with adults, and each style teaches him something different. Children help each other achieve increased degrees of sophistication. For example, children learn from other children by talking with and watching one another, by trying new scenarios, and by exchanging information, even fantasies.

In the earliest stages, little ones play merely in proximity to others, without being involved with them. They play alone and find satisfying activities for themselves. As they grow, they learn to share toys, give them away, and fight over them.

When children enter nursery schools, child-care programs, parent cooperatives, or have visits away from home, they are introduced to new children, different toys and playthings, and other styles of playing. As they discover how to handle these situations, children strengthen their confidence and gain new maturity.

## Power of Play

Because of the power of play, you must understand your child's need to explore, to meet and play with other children, and you must try not to interfere with your little one's activity. Instead, serve as your child's Play Tutor—observe, enhance, and augment her experiences.

When playtime is ending, for example, it is important to give the child enough advance notice so she can have time to bring the activity to a satisfying close. If we respect our children's playtime, the child is almost always more cooperative when she must change gears to eat, nap, or go elsewhere.

In play, children gain mastery over themselves and learn their own power in relationships with others. They grasp social values such as biases and responsibilities. They communicate better. They absorb concepts like making judgments. Each child expresses a unique style of play and the ways he plays when he is young reflect how he will deal with others during later life.

Allow your child to select his own form of play, as his choices are important for his individual growth. Rigid rules can be a damper to natural self-expression. As parent and Play Tutor, honor your offspring's early learning domain. Inherent to this is providing appropriate skill-building toys.

## Advantages of Play

Play experiences help the child to:

- Gain an understanding of the world.
- Act productively with other children and adults.
- Get and hold the attention of others in a suitable way.
- Enhance the ability to concentrate, an essential skill before he begins school.
- Expand his natural curiosity, whet his ability to solve problems, and foster spontaneity. These are each central components of mastering the learning process.

When children enjoy what they are doing (provided what they are doing is positive behavior), there is less need for your discipline or your worry. If they are having fun, children can play with blocks, construct buildings, or play with other children in mutual cooperative activities for long periods of time.

Adults sometimes forget the importance of play. Through their play, children tell us what they are thinking and how they are feeling. If there are problems their play will reveal them. Play Therapy is an important way to treat children who are having difficulty with traumas, emotional issues, or other problems. You can better understand your child if you listen and watch her at play.

Before you look at the different ways your child can use toys, and before you become conversant with finding the right toys, I would like you to first think about the important place toys have held in your own life.

I created the following "Childhood-Toy Memory Exercise" for

my many workshops with parents and teachers. It works well alone or with a partner. If you are doing it alone you may want to tape the questions slowly and then replay them with your eyes closed. If you are doing it with a partner each should take a turn at trying the exercise. Through the experience you will discover that, no matter how "adult" you are, the significance of certain toys and play events often remains vivid in your life.

Read this next section out loud. After asking a question allow plenty of time for you and/or your partner to think and for various childhood images to emerge. If you are doing the process alone, put the tape on pause.

## DR. TOY'S CHILDHOOD-TOY MEMORY EXERCISE

Close your eyes. Get comfortable and relax. Take a deep breath. You and/or your partner says the following:

"Let us return to your early memories.

"Imagine yourself as a child. Imagine yourself at play. Do you see yourself inside the house or outside in the yard? Can you remember a toy you played with frequently? Can you see that toy?

"What is your toy's color? Shape? Size? Can you smell it? Can you hold it and turn it over easily in your hand?

"Is it large? Small? Are you holding it tightly?

"Are you playing by yourself or with other children? Can you remember how long that toy held your interest?

"Did anyone try to take your toy from you? How did you feel?

"Did you play with that toy for a long time?

"Do you still have that toy today in your treasured collection of childhood things? What happened to that toy?

"Open your eyes, and take a deep breath."

At this time think about the pictures evoked and think about or discuss what you remember with your partner.

Amazing, isn't it? That special toy you played with as a child still, for many of you, remains vivid in your memory. If a few of you do not have such recollections that, too, is significant. The *lack* of toys or memories of them affects us, too! Perhaps after this exercise you will better understand how important the toys are with which children play.

Toys (or their absence) are a formative part of childhood. Strong memories arise as soon as you allow your mind to return to your early years.

Sometimes those memories are painful ones of loss or anger. Many adults can remember the feelings of having a greatly loved doll or teddy bear suddenly pulled away or broken by a brother or sister. Or, perhaps, the memory is of never having owned a stuffed animal to cuddle. Long afterward they can still remember the pain of that experience, and their adult behavior and/or attitudes will reflect it.

If you recognize that you might have some disturbing feelings from childhood, endeavor to examine what happened. Try to forgive your parents, siblings, or friend for doing something that might have hurt you. Put that pain in perspective, and allow it to fade from your memories. In that way you will be able to move ahead with your current life and responsibilities. If this approach doesn't work and something is still troubling you, seek counseling. Getting to the bottom of it and working through old pain will allow you to fully enjoy the pleasure of playing with your own child, rather than using her as a substitute for your own childhood.

There are the happy recollections, too. Many people report the fun of building with their Erector sets, making towering creations, or building their first train ensemble that impressed younger brothers and sisters. You may be surprised to know that pride in such accomplishments can last long into adulthood!

Childhood is full of magical moments: receiving that first dress-up doll, setting up the tracks of that first train (or watching Dad take over!), learning to play jacks and ball, jumping rope, doing tricks with your yo-yo, sailing a wooden boat on a pond, having an afternoon tea party with dolls and little teacups, and cooking over your little toy stove.

These are some of the vivid pictures, fondly recalled, that rush by when adults watch their own baby in his crib. Their new baby

## SOME QUESTIONS TO ASK YOURSELF ABOUT TOYS IN YOUR CHILDHOOD

- Did you have a lot of different toys to play with?
- Did you have to share them with other children?
- When you went to preschool were there ample toys?
- Did you have good experiences with new playthings that you had never seen before?
- Were you able to figure out how to play with such items yourself?
- Did your parents help you figure it out?
- Did your parents ask you to be quiet often? Did you have a place where you could play?
- Did your toys break easily or did they last for many years?
- Did you enjoy playing with many toys? Only a few? Did you use toys to play games?
- Did your toys make you imagine wonderful things?
- Is a particular toy the reason you are now involved in a job or a hobby?
- Did you have a hobby or a special skill that you enjoyed? Do you now?
- Was there a special doll or train that you cherished?
- Do you remember building with blocks and construction toys?

playing with his toes or with their fingers, or trying to catch light coming through the window, sparks scenes from the parents' own childhood.

What toys will *you* provide to create those enchanting moments for your precious infant's future joy?

Certainly the basic function of any toy is to give pleasure to a child. Whether high-tech or old-fashioned, toys open exciting doors to fresh awareness. So, before evaluating or thinking about toys for your young one, try to think back to your own times with toys. It will strengthen the empathy you have—and need—for your child.

If you do remember many of these experiences, then toys were important in your childhood. You have an appreciation for toys, a good memory, and you were an active player. You probably still are. So enjoy the rest of this book, and the playtimes you will have with your child in what can be a fun "second childhood."

## Power of Memories

Independently several architects have told me that playing with blocks as a child helped influence them toward their career choice—building with bigger and better blocks. Teachers told me how they can remember the fun of playing "school" and making a decision to teach. Writers recall creating fantasy dramas: tales of derring-do with roles for everyone—even the dog.

Have you ever made a connection like that?

You have the opportunity to enrich your child with similar, powerful inspirations. You can provide your child with new sensations that do not rely just on products you buy, but on the high value you place on *playtime*. Creative playtime, whether it be with a stick a child has picked up in the park or a hundred-dollar high-tech game, is what is really meaningful. *How* the child plays and *what* he gets out of it are what's paramount, not the cost of the plaything.

A parent's role is a complex one: so many books to read, so many things to do and be responsible for—food, clothing, health. Equally complex is your child's social development. Of course, playtime is one area that provides the most fun, relaxation, entertainment—and educational socialization—for everyone.

During playtime, you can help your little one imagine whole new worlds. Throughout her life, such activities will stimulate her creativity, her sense of humor, her sense of balance and proportion, wonder, reasoning, social development, and much more.

As I examine with you the different stages of development and suggest types of toys for each stage, you will learn basic techniques to encourage your child appropriately. You will also receive many tips on how to clean toys, store them, shop, recycle, and otherwise become a knowledgeable Play Tutor.

## FINDING PLAYTHINGS

These days, going into any toy store can be overwhelming. So many shelves are filled with choices in every category! There are so many varieties today that any single store has great difficulty stocking all of them. The store's buyer has to discriminate and make careful selections. So do you.

To find the right kind of toys, you will have to visit different toy stores, department stores, gift stores, search catalogs, and the internet and find stores handling secondhand, recycled toys.

You may start your search by visiting our World Wide Web site (http://www.drtoy.com) on the Internet. *Dr. Toy's Guide* is our on-line magazine which offers articles about most kinds of toys and provides descriptions of hundreds of our selected best, award-winning products, including toys, books, software, tapes, and more. A customer-service number is provided for each item so that you can find a store near you to help locate it. You may also refer to Dr. Toy's Play Resources in the back of this book for a selected list of suggested companies and the 800 number of ASTRA, the

American Specialty Toy Retailing Association, for specific locations nearest you.

I have carefully evaluated numerous items throughout the year to narrow the choices for the annual "100 Best Children's Products" awards and the results are found in the *Guide*. *Dr. Toy's Guide* includes features about after-school and vacation items, classic toys, and many other kinds of toys and play products. This service is free.

Alternatively, you may write for a current listing of this same information by sending a self-addressed stamped #10 envelope to 268 Bush Street, San Francisco, California, 94104. Please include any questions you may have about toys and we will respond in our King Features Syndicate column "Dr. Toy." Look for it in your local paper.

## The Wish List

Look at the different types of playthings. Match them to your child's skills and interests. For example:

- Construction products help develop dexterity and building skills.
- Board games help children cooperate and learn with their friends. With your guidance they can also teach how to compete positively and how to deal well with losing.
- Puppets help develop language skills and hand/eye coordination.

I suggest that when you shop for toys you take your child along at least once a year, but avoid the preholiday frenzy. Make an outing of it. Let him show you the things he likes. You will hear about items he's seen on TV or talked over with friends. Let him create a "wish list." Get him involved in the selection process.

Still, prepare your young one carefully ahead of time so he knows that everything that attracts his attention may not necessarily be purchased. The skill of saying "no" gently but firmly—and *sticking* to it—is possibly a parent's greatest challenge.

For the child under three, analyze what she needs before going to the store. Her attention span is short, so you will want to narrow the different choices into specific categories. Give her the choice among two or three possibilities. Gather a few possibilities and then ask her, for example, "Which puzzle do you like?" Screen the products with the help of my guidelines. Giving your child several options is important to her learning process. This helps her become more discerning and self-confident by allowing her free choice while you exercise the necessary control over what she chooses *from*. By giving her choices, you show that you trust her judgment and she will become more confident and a more discerning and knowledgeable consumer.

In each chapter we will discuss specific things to look for when selecting toys for each stage of a child's growth, but there are some basic points that you should remember for any toy that you buy.

## Shopping Guidelines

What are some of the qualities to look for when selecting a good product?

**DESIGN.** The product must have been tested carefully by the manufacturer with the intended age group. The best possible materials should have been used in assembly. The item should be durable. The toy should be easy for the child to use and to keep clean.

**QUALITY.** Consider what materials are used to make the article. Is the product appealing in color, shape, and workmanship? We expect to get what we pay for but, unfortunately, sometimes this is not true and we are disappointed.

**DURABILITY.** How long will the selection last? Is it childproof? Can it be easily broken? A plaything should be long lasting, substantial, and made of good materials.

**SAFETY.** The toy must be tested by the manufacturer and by an independent laboratory. It must meet U.S. Consumer Product Safety Commission standards, the U.S. Government Standards of Safety requirements. See more details on toy safety later in this chapter and throughout the book.

**PLAY VALUE.** You will want a product that lasts as long as possible and has many different and long-lasting uses. Good examples of toys with high play value are blocks, construction toys, and yo-yos. The item should have clear instructions so you and your child are guided to its best use by the designer and the manufacturer.

**APPROPRIATENESS.** The toy must fulfill the usual play patterns for the child's age. Products that are too complex are easily frustrating. Toys that are too easy are boring. When necessary, show the child how to use the plaything properly. It's best, however, to allow your child to discover how to use the product himself, depending on his age and ability.

# DR. TOY'S PRODUCT GUIDELINES

Another important way to look at toys is by evaluating their *active*, *creative*, and *educational* features.

*Active* playthings improve the child's physical activity and exercise. They help develop large and small muscles, hand/eye coordination, dexterity, and encourage children to learn and practice climbing, crawling, and improving balance.

Items that assist in active play include balls, bicycles, blocks, skates, punching bags, jump ropes, pounding toys, and ride-ons. Other active products include construction toys, adventure props, and manipulatives such as puzzles. Children do enjoy "destructive" play, which means breaking down or mixing up things like sand, clay, or blocks. Kids like to build up, take apart, and punch things. Why not? It's fun!

*Creative* toys stimulate the child's imagination at all levels. She can experience surprise, can expand her thinking, and she will be encouraged in self-expression.

Examples of creative toy products are blocks, crafts, dollhouses, mirrors, musical instruments, puppets, stuffed animals, and art supplies. You will also want to select items to foster the child's dramatic ability, social skills, and artistic development. Puppets, games, and cooperative activities help children to interact with each other, while being considerate and taking turns may be fostered with baby dolls and jump ropes.

The *educational* attributes of a toy help a child learn specific skills, and sometimes several skills at once. Any toy can be educational if the child's shown how to use it in an enriching way. The right object can help with reading and writing, and can build skills which prepare the child for science and counting. You will want a balance of playthings to stimulate your child's mental abilities, challenge his thinking, and help him in problem-solving.

Some items which contribute in the educational arena are board games, blocks, books, checkers, construction toys, Peg-Boards, puzzles, science projects, hobbies (stamps or coin collecting), software, CDs, audio- and videotapes, microscopes, telescopes, and other special equipment.

Certainly you, as Play Tutor, must think about future school participation, after-school activities, vacation times, sickness, and other encounters the child will have. How can you assure that the toys he plays with now will help ready him for future demands? The answers are in this book.

Some basic questions to ask before you buy any toy:

## DR. TOY'S TIPS ON SELECTING TOYS AND OTHER CHILDREN'S PRODUCTS

1. **Is the toy safe?** Are there any potential hazards? Is the product too small? Any sharp edges or loose ties? Is it nontoxic? Durable? Will it take rough treatment? Does it meet Consumer Product Safety Standards? Is there a guarantee on the product?

2. **Is the product fun?** A toy or children's product is supposed to entertain the child. It should amuse, delight, excite, and be enjoyable.

3. **Is the product appropriate?** Is this toy or product significant now? Does it fit the child's age, skills, and abilities? Will it hold his interest? Will he use the product happily?

4. **Is the product well designed?** Is it easy to use? Does it look good? Feel good?

5. **Is the product versatile?** Is there more than one use for the product?

6. **Is the product durable?** Will it be something that will last a long time? Children play hard and subject their toys to a lot of abuse and wear.

7. **Is the product enticing to the child?** Does it offer an opportunity for fun, to learn, and to think? Does it help her learn about her living environment? Is the toy or product inviting?

8. **Will the product help the child expand his creativity?** With the right products the child can expand his imagination in art, crafts, hobbies, language, reading, music, movement, and drama.

9. **Will the toy frustrate or challenge the child?** Does the toy offer something new to learn, to practice, or to try? Will the child know how to use the product? Or will it be too difficult to use without adult assistance?

10. **Does the product match the package and the package match the product?** If the toy does not

match ads or packaging it can be disappointing. Is age-grading clear? Is the item in the store like the product shown in the print or TV advertisement?

11. **Will the toy help nurture childhood?** Does the product help the child express emotions, experience concern for others, practice positive social interaction? Does it provide value to her childhood? Or are there any violent, sexist, or other negative aspects to the product?

12. **What will the toy teach?** Does it help expand positive self-esteem, values, understanding, cultural awareness? Does it offer practice in skill-building? Hand/eye coordination? Fine- and large-motor skills? Communication? Does it educate the child about the environment? The community? The world? About history? Computers? Other skills?

13. **Can the product be cleaned and reused?** If it is not washable, can it be cleaned in some practical way?

14. **Can I afford this toy?** Does the price match the value received?

## Dr. Toy's Safety Tips

When selecting toys you want to be certain that all safety standards have been met. Check that the toy's age range on the package is appropriate for your child. Make a note about the manufacturer and the name of the product in your Playbook (described on page 23). If the company has a customer-service number, jot it down. If there is any problem you can report it or call for replacement information.

Be especially careful about objects designed for children under three years. Protect your toddler in every way, not only with the toys you buy, but also with tiny things in the house he can grab and put in his mouth.

The following tips are important; please review them carefully and keep your child's safety in mind at all times.

## DR. TOY'S SAFETY TIPS ON TOYS

To make your child's toys safe be sure to check for these potential problems before you buy a toy and recheck all of your child's toys from time to time:

- No sharp edges.
- No loose ties.
- No little pieces that can be loosened.
- No small objects for children under three.
- Always confirm any paint like finger paints is nontoxic.
- Check reliability of the company and store where you purchase your toy.
- Buy toys from a store that you know and trust.
- Buy from a company that guarantees its product and confirms that each product produced has been carefully tested for being appropriate to your child's developmental stage.

Problems with a toy should be brought to the store's attention. Tell the manager about any defects; the store will want to know. If the toy is faulty you should obtain a refund or be helped to locate a substitute. Remember to keep receipts.

## The Economics of Toys

Toys can be expensive. Buying good toys, however, does not have to cost a fortune if you select carefully. Purchasing a lot of things that only sit around unused makes no sense. You want interest and use. You want to be economical and buy smart. Use your time for wise toy-buying. You can provide your child with many experiences that do not dent your pocketbook.

Some toys will be used over and over again and you will discover that these toys are meeting some special needs in your son or daughter. Items that become ragged with use over the years (with great resistance to their being replaced!) are often stuffed animals, a doll—perhaps a rag doll like Raggedy Ann—and certain books. Action toys like scooters, a wagon, or a sled are given up reluctantly as the child's size increases.

Such playthings prorate to a negligible cost over the years, but more importantly, their value *increases* far beyond any dollar amount. For example:

- Your child's *emotional* development will be enhanced when he plays with soft, cuddly toys.
- *Mentally*, she will be strengthened when she has a variety of books to stretch her mind.
- *Physically*, she will be empowered when she has a push-pull toy to walk and steer ahead of herself.
- *Creatively*, he can grow when he uses finger or water paints with which to color.

In addition to toys, many objects around the house can be used for learning, such as measuring cups, pots and pans, wooden spoons, plastic bowls, or such complementary things as fabric, shells, and pinecones, which make for lots of merriment and are inexpensive playthings.

For example, you can drape an intriguing, washable fabric on an old bridge table and create a great playhouse.

Shells and pinecones are great props for that handmade shack built on a desert island after a shipwreck.

The dining-room chairs, tip-tilted in strategic ways, form a wonderful castle or, perhaps, Merlin's cave.

Play itself does not cost money. Play is built on common sense and imagination.

## Toys Teach

Consider these examples of the way toys teach:

- The child's first sense of color, shapes, sizes, and weights comes from manipulating products like Puzzle House or ShapeMakers.
- Children test and figure things out with projects like assembling models.
- The child learns concentration playing card games.
- While playing with blocks, the child gains skills needed for reading and math. He also learns about balance and selection—decision-making by shape and size. And he learns about the need to adapt and to be flexible when he realizes he must make changes. He is also being creative and adaptive in fitting pieces together in new forms and shapes.
- Foam bats or bop bags are useful in showing an acceptable way to ventilate angry or frustrated feelings.
- Sorting, choosing, trying various shaped puzzle pieces and puzzle blocks heightens understanding of dissimilar sizes and how they can relate. This activity also gives significance to differentiating colors.
- Games such as ring toss improve dexterity and focus.
- Puppets expand communication skills.
- Board games can improve social skills.
- Books expand information, imagination, and understanding.
- To fine-tune artistic talent, art supplies, craft kits, and/or creative software programs are good choices.
- A child's competitive spirit—a vital survival tool—is enhanced by a computer or positive video games. They're a lot of fun, too.

# TOY STORAGE

Once you have purchased your young one's toys, the next challenge is to find the best place to store them so that they are neat and reasonably organized.

## DR. TOY'S TIPS ON TOY STORAGE AND USE

- Toys should be easily accessible to the child.
- Boxes can hold a lot of toys. Label them so it's easy to determine the contents, or use clear boxes for quick identification.
- Create sturdy shelves to hold boxes, games, and larger toys.
- A hammock is great for storing stuffed animals, or a clothesline (with clothespins that snap open) can be hung from the ceiling or across a corner.
- If you buy a toy chest, be sure it has a safety lock. Children have been caught inside chests and been unable to get out. Some toy chests can also be difficult for a young child to reach into and out of. It is preferable to have open shelves where their toys can be easily seen, handled, and returned.
- Do not have too many toys and games cluttering the floor; it can be dangerous. If toys are easy to find and easy to put away, it will be more agreeable to your child to take care of them. They will last longer and your offspring will have much less frustration when she wants to find something.
- Children can learn to put toys away. This skill, part of Montessori's teaching principles, is an important lesson. It's a good way for your young one to learn responsibility.
- Occasionally recirculate the toys for fresh play so your child doesn't get bored. (It's also a good way to renew your child's interest in old toys.)

# THE PLAYBOOK

Consider keeping a "Playbook"—a notebook with ideas that apply to *your* child and tips from your reading and research. You can keep notes also of observations you make of your child's play, her favorite activities, her "wish list," and favorite toys. You might record birthday gifts and who gave them, and funny tidbits you want to remember years from now. You can keep photos of special toys and of your child playing with them.

Be sure to note the places where you were able to purchase the best toys. This would be a good place to store your receipts and keep a list of the names of manufacturers you have found reliable.

# OBSERVING CHILDREN PLAY

As has been mentioned, a parent who watches play patterns is versed in the child's changing play needs.

Playtime does not depend on toys or anything else. Watch kittens, puppies, baby monkeys—they are full of play. Watch your young child excitedly chase a butterfly, follow a leaf, or pick up a stick and transform it into a magic wand.

Play depends upon the young person's willingness to experience her improvisations. It is her spirit—her inner being—that suggests unexpected twists and turns in her perceptions, that creates her laughter and funny faces, that turns a simple rock into a toad, a twig into an elf, a gesture into a regal dismissal of courtiers.

Stimulate your little girl to draw from her inner self and infuse her playthings with her imagination. Provide her with boxes and unusual props. They can give her a "warm-up" for more sophisticated playthings.

Here are a few guidelines that apply to all children at play. You will find more specific information as we discuss types of products for each age.

## DR. TOY'S TIPS ON CHILD OBSERVATION

- Observe what occurs in your child's play and write down important events in your Playbook.
- Watch how he shares and how he plays with others.
- How does she use toys? Is there a favorite she returns to? Encourage curiosity and initiative. Does she find new uses for her toys?
- Watch how your child masters skills. Does he take time to discover new ways to play? Is he impatient or easily distracted?
- Does your child follow directions? Does she use ingenuity?
- Notice the types of toys with which he spends the most time. What does he most like to do with them? What does he not like?

Expand your child's playing repertoire. You may do this by introducing new toys gradually and allowing her to explore and discover new things. In the case of games she will need your assistance at first to learn to play by the rules. It's fun to engage in Candy Land, Monopoly, Parcheesi, Othello, Scrabble, checkers, or chess with your child.

Many toys are created for the child's own self-discovery. Toys like LEGOs, Erector sets, Lincoln Logs, and wooden blocks open up hours of imaginative entertainment and pride of achievement.

Your child has the ability to manipulate, to experiment, and to try new things. Children learn best in the early years by trial and error, observation and comparison, and discovery of their own abilities and those of others they may want to emulate.

Help your child be a good player, to take turns, to share, to learn how to win and to lose. Whether as a child or when grown to adulthood, a person who is a good loser and who does not quit

## DR. TOY'S CHECKLIST TO HELP YOUR CHILD BEST USE TOYS AND PLAY PRODUCTS

- Allow your child to discover the toy and explore it fully. Do not interfere, even when she makes "mistakes," unless frustration sets in.
- Check on toys frequently to be sure nothing is broken.
- Create a space for your child to have his own play area.
- Give your child time to replace the toys she's used.
- Make sure you have a good mix of toy types and other play products.
- Be careful that there are not too many playthings out which may confuse the child.
- Encourage your offspring to balance play with time to read and to exercise.
- Be a playmate when it fits, and nourish communication skills.
- If your child is going to play with a board game, be sure he understands the rules of the game. This is a perfect time for you both to play and talk with each other.
- If batteries are required, be sure they are on hand and operating. Test them. Show your child how to turn off the toy if it does not do that automatically.
- Have fun together every day and enjoy her unique gifts. Notice and appreciate your child's creative use of toys.

is always a winner. A good loser is not just being a good sport; a good loser exerts confidence and knows that "losing" is just a temporary setback. If he keeps on playing he is on his way to ultimate success. Discovering this is a lesson in fortitude and stamina all kids need to master.

When you instill a sense of fun in your youngster, you open her eyes to the most powerful of long-term goals: the eagerness and the motivation to absorb knowledge. To learn!

A child who plays well is being prepared for academic learning. If he has had a strong, happy, and productive playtime when young, he will be a better student, prepared to make the most of his education. He will have improved concentration, be more focused, and be able to express himself well orally and in writing.

If, for example, you have a personal, well-established reading habit, and if you also read every day to your young child, she will enjoy books. Keep in mind that in this era children are exposed to fast-moving information and exponentially advancing technology. Sometimes it is difficult to get her just to sit down and focus on reading. You need to set the example. Turn off the TV and turn on her mind! When you have to be away, make a tape of her favorite story. She will love listening to your voice as she follows it in the book (much to the delight of your baby-sitter).

You might ask your little one's grandparents to tape stories and send the tape along with the books they read. What a delight to have granny nearby, even when she can't be there to read before bedtime.

We want our children to be emotionally resilient, stable, and smart. Use their playtime to achieve this.

## You Are Your Child's First Big Toy!

Throughout infancy and childhood, it is how you play with your children, what you do together, and your playfulness and positive responses to their questions that are the crux of their emotional health, well-being, and self-confidence.

"The family that plays together, stays together," and has lots more joy together! Keep in mind the real reason, perhaps, for having children. Do your best to give your children happy childhoods. Help them grow and become stable, responsible adults who do not lose their balance, good humor, or joie de vivre. Recall your childhood memories that keep you in touch with your own child's world. Your long-term hopes for your child will enable her favorite Big Toy to be the best toy of all!

## Every Day Is Playtime

Remember that your child needs time every day to play. If possible, join him for short periods as you can. In the long run, your child will be happier, brighter, and your relationship will be much better. My daughter, now a young adult with a child of her own, still enjoys playing musical tapes, sharing a board game, and reading excerpts aloud from books. However, as we laugh together we both keep a close eye on her growing son as he rapidly discovers new objects to play with and I find I'm now sharing with my daughter the experiences I had when she was little. There is, I think, not much greater bliss than this.

Perhaps you are a collector of toys: dolls, trains, teddy bears, dollhouses, miniatures. Collecting such childhood treasures is a great delight. So, as you find wonderful toys for your child, think about getting a few special ones for yourself! Wise executives and parents know that a small toy can do wonders for stressful afternoons when one must take some time out. Play recharges the batteries. Look for that executive yo-yo the next time you are in your favorite toy store.

Everyone can enjoy toys—now is the perfect time to learn.

# TWO

# Baby

## BIRTH TO ONE YEAR

Becoming a first-time parent is one of life's great, stirring experiences, and the first toys for your precious new baby are very special. Most "ladies-in-waiting" and papas-to-be enjoy shopping, looking for ways to set up and decorate the baby's area, and planning the playthings to buy the new infant. It's often hard to be practical about these purchases. Many of us, in the thrill of brand-new parenthood, tend to overdo the number, suitability, even the size of things we buy beforehand.

When Tom and Arlene learned they were to have a baby, Tom wanted to celebrate immediately. He rushed to the nearest toy store and purchased what he wanted most, a large set of LEGO blocks, something he had never gotten to play with as a child. Actually, the time he took to use the new LEGOs relaxed him and satisfied his own unmet childhood needs. From the set, he created a large animal to decorate his baby's room and proudly installed it on a shelf.

Although it was a while before Annie, his two-year-old daughter, got to play with her first starter set of LEGO DUPLOs, her daddy had lots of fun with his own set. During the two years after Annie's birth, Tom and Arlene learned to shop more selectively. They have made wise purchases of toys that can be used also by their second child, whom they expect soon.

It's a given—grown-ups buy toys for kids, even little babies, with which they themselves would like to play!

You are your baby's Play Tutor, so select those first toys carefully and be guided by the baby's basic abilities and needs. As he grows, these expand and change. Watch him explore, observe his responses, and use the development guides in this book to interpret his behavior. Each child is unique, of course, and often acts differently from the "average" as described for his age.

Pay close attention to the age range on toy packages. These will usually serve to guide you on appropriateness. However, *you* are the final authority on your little one. Do not rush her into activities she is not ready for or, on the other hand, don't limit her to age ranges she's obviously beyond. You have been observing her behavior, interacting with her, and have read about how her development relates to the toys you choose for her. Trust yourself.

## Baby's First Big Toy

If you accept that you are the most important Big Toy in your baby's life, the one special person who will feed, talk to, sing with, stroke, bathe, and play with him, and also your baby's first contact with the world, then you can see how important it is to take good care of yourself physically and emotionally, before, during, and after pregnancy.

## Preparing for the Coming Event

Having clear communication between you and your mate will help resolve many of the questions. Before your baby arrives, it is vitally important that you are both prepared with good health, good attitudes, and reasonable expectations.

To prepare for your baby, visit friends and learn what toys, activities, and ideas have worked for them. Start your Playbook (see page 23). Enter notes from your reading, and benefit from the extensive research in child growth and development. New information has led to improved guidelines, more books, excellent toys, and the increased production of carefully tested products.

Make a useful and inexpensive toy or two for your new baby. Easy step-by-step instructions and patterns for creating them are available in good crafts books. Even making but one special toy will be a cheerful project and get you pleasantly through days of waiting. For those of you who have never been into knitting, sewing, or carpentry, you might find that waiting for this new life is a different kind of time.

For example, a simple sock puppet is easy to make, especially for "noncraftsy" people, and it will charm your little one for a long time.

For the more experienced (or those determined to become so), consider creating a rag-crocheted doll, or teddy bear. A knitted stuffed unicorn or kitten to cuddle will warm baby in many more ways than one, and for more years than you'd expect.

In your Playbook, start a Baby Gift List. When people ask what gift to give the newest family member, consult your notes to advise them. Create a record of presents. In one column, list the toy or indicate if a check was received, and record the name of the person who gave the item. You might also wish to include information such as the date you received the gift and the date that the thank-you note was sent.

Your thank-you note should always specifically mention the toy and comment on the child's reaction (favorable, of course). As a particularly thoughtful gesture, why not send along a photograph of your baby, if possible, with the toy (and keep a print for the Playbook, too)? If the gift was money, include a photo of the toy it purchased. The picture will be a special treasure to the gift-giver, and it is a rewarding expression of your appreciation.

# Early Shopping for the Baby

Timing is important. Giving something to your infant before she is ready for it will lead only to frustration, disappointment, or boredom. You may want to run right out and start buying a shelfful of dolls as soon as you learn that baby's on the way, but it's probably more sensible to purchase a soft, washable, baby-proof bunny rabbit or stuffed teddy bear instead. Dolls (except a certain kind I'll tell you about later in this chapter and, of course, the soft one you created yourself) will come later, when your child will most appreciate them.

Your rag doll—the one you made—is different. It is soft and textured, but most of all your smell is woven into it with your own hands and will bring a new baby comfort when you must be away from her crib.

## Active, Creative, and Educational Toys for Baby

Three main categories of toys are the basis of your child's "smart play": toys that keep him *active*, toys that spur him to *create*, and toys that *educate*. Many good toys have qualities that comprise more than one of these categories and do not lend themselves to rigid classification. Your own creativeness can merge these different functions into a toy. Also, it's not necessary in every case to separate toys into those for girls or boys, as many items satisfy the needs of both.

In this chapter I shall suggest playthings based on the purposes for which the product has been designed. For example, when you are confronted with a dozen choices of well-made rattles manufactured by a dozen different companies, which one do you choose? Use my guidelines, and when you make your selection consider the reasons you want the item, then observe what happens when the baby takes it, and be influenced in your further choices by his responses.

The most useful guidance I supply is to give you ideas on the best playthings for each age and suggest uses for them, and also to mention a few companies as examples. If I do not list a specific company, it does not mean its toys are not good. It may simply be that I have not yet examined the products closely.

Specific brand-name toys are not predominate in my recommendations. You will have a sampling of good ideas in each category with a few suggested manufacturers. Your toy store should be able to supply you with examples in each category. If the specific type you seek is not in stock, it can be ordered for you.

Don't forget to take lots of pictures during this first year. Photographs taken of your baby and the objects he plays with will bring both of you enjoyment and delight in the future.

## Baby Is Ready for Gentle Play

Your baby is born with all of the senses necessary for play. She sees, hears, tastes, touches, and smells. During this period your baby observes, experiments, and begins to master her environment. She absorbs sensations that prepare her for playthings—hearing your voice, hearing laughter and music; feeling shapes and textures like papa's head, mama's nose, brother's woolly sweater; tasting dad's linen shirt and mom's wedding ring; and seeing lamp lights, blanket shadows, movement. She smells her soap, the pine tree outside her window, her mother's aroma, her father's jogging sweats, and her brother's peanut-butter snack.

The way you and baby's family play with her from the very beginning determines how effectively she will play when she's older. Babies who feel secure and confident reach out for pleasure and stimulation and for positive relationships. Babies who are denied such gentle fun soon withdraw and show signs of fear, lack of confidence, nonresponsiveness, and worse. From the moment of birth, the way a baby is treated affects him for the rest of his life.

The infant picks up subliminal cues from his senses. The newborn's tactile sense and hearing are, for now, the most highly developed, although tasting, smelling, and vision advance swiftly. Therefore, touch the new baby in ways that are pleasant and soothing: give him mild, nonenergetic baths; carry him close; snuggle with him; rock him; sing to him; wrap him in soft, warm blankets; and gently talk and whisper to him.

Studies have proved that breast-feeding brings the mother and her baby closer. In addition to the practical function of providing nutrition and immunities, breast-feeding provides tactile stimulation. Regardless of feeding method—breast or bottle—feeding time is a perfect period for heightened communication between mother and child. Ashley Montagu in his book, *Touching*, strongly endorses touch as essential emotional support. Other psychologists such as Dr. James Prescott reinforce this theory with extensive cross-cultural research. Babies that are not touched do not do well mentally or in other ways that are essential for healthy growth.

And so the baby first learns about love and about trust from the primitive responses of her senses. She next sifts these responses into meaning: She does not merely see, she observes; she does not merely hear noise, she differentiates sounds. The first month the infant will be sleeping and eating most of the time. She turns to light and sound sources, but abrupt or loud sounds frighten the baby and should be avoided.

Because the newborn is exceptionally sensitive to sound, if a loud, sharp noise like a door slamming does not startle him, consult a pediatrician about the possibility of a hearing impairment.

The baby has come from a prolonged period in a protected, dark, quiet place into a bright and noisy world. Because her eyes are not able to focus the first few weeks, it is difficult for her to follow moving objects precisely. At first she detects only shades of gray and white. Soon she begins to separate colors and they hold absolute allure for her.

Gradually your little one learns to focus his eyes on the designs of the ceiling and walls. As he approaches four and five weeks old, he is more aware of his surroundings; his eyes focus and the objects in his crib become more important.

A colorful mobile, with or without a music box, will attract

## EARLY TOYS

| | | |
|---|---|---|
| 1. Bath toys (use one to three) | (A) | give tactile stimulation; focus attention span; work as distracter so you can bathe him |
| 2. Mobile | (E) | promotes eye focus; builds attention span |
| 3. Music boxes and tape recorders | (A) | for auditory stimulation and soothing when fussy; relax you, too |
| 4. Rattles | (A) | improve sound awareness; attention span; provide tactile stimulation |
| 5. Stuffed toys | (AC) | help tactile refinement |

baby now. She responds to a rattle, to your smiles, and she turns toward sounds. She laughs and makes gurgling sounds. Music will fascinate her (although her attention span is still very short).

By six weeks your infant will stare happily at an object which moves slowly in the wind. He perks up when he hears people, telephones, doorbells. He looks into mother's and father's eyes, and smiles. The baby will move his arms and legs, but cannot grasp or hold on to objects for very long. His eyes are moving, beginning to coordinate, and he can follow a toy moving slowly in front of him.

Your newborn's favorite position when in bed is lying on her back, with legs drawn up and head turned to the side. During the early months, newborns can best focus on objects about eight to twelve inches from their eyes.

You might introduce pictures to your infant, containing interesting objects such as a face or a flower. A very young baby is most attracted to pictures of simple shapes which contrast sharply against the background. Baby tends to look at the outlines of the shape rather than at the center. As he grows, he will look more at the center of the picture and notice detail. He will begin to look at very simple pictures for shorter periods of time and concentrate longer on more complex pictures. Talk to him as he looks at each picture, and let your voice and body action, together with your words, tell baby more about the picture. Attention span is very short in the early months so make these sessions brief—only a few minutes. Your conversations are the most important part of the time together.

## TOY SUGGESTIONS FOR BABIES IN THE FIRST SIX WEEKS

**A** CTIVE (promotes hand/eye coordination, muscle tone, strength)
**C** REATIVE (encourages spontaneity, self-expression)
**E** DUCATIONAL (challenges thinking, mental growth)

### 1. Bath Toys

Bath time should be a happy, relaxed time and can be more so with the addition of a few simple bath toys. Water play adds a new dimension to tactile experiences. Bath toys—soft, pliable rubber and plastic shapes, like a rubber ducky—are fun. Floating turtles and fish will delight your baby when you squeeze them and surprise her with a blurpy, squirty sound. She'll love splashing and reaching out to grasp squishy playthings bobbing in the water.

You might use a colorful clean sponge or bath mitt to wash

baby, then let her have it to squeeze and play with. The mitt can easily become a little puppet for a few minutes and will make baby laugh if you talk as a puppet character. My daughter used to giggle a lot when I did this and she delighted in the improvised bathmate.

Bath toys also work well when you and baby play on a warm day with water in the backyard. Keep baby in your arms at all times, even in small play pools, and if any water is directed at him, it must only be a very soft splash or extremely gentle spray.

Good bath toys are made by Battat, Chicco, Fisher-Price, and PlaySkool. $2–10.

## 2. Mobile

The mobile is a series of objects held together by two crossbars and extended cords that move slowly in the air currents. It provides visual focus for baby during his first months, when the mobile is attached firmly to the crib rail so that he can look up at it. Move it from one side of the crib to the other to offer variety. In the first two months raise the apparatus as baby grows—always keeping it out of reach.

A mobile design in black and white with emphasis on movement and a few simple shapes is appropriate for the first eight weeks, as babies do not see colors clearly but do notice simple structures. You may want to try a variety of mobiles, and alternate them or hang them in separate places around the room.

Baby watches the hanging objects intently at about a foot distance from her (figures of animals, fairy-story characters, flowers, small balls, even abstractions). She strengthens her eye focus and learns to concentrate as she follows the movements of the shapes above her.

After two months, look for a mobile with sharp color contrasts. It should still have simple figures that are easy for the baby to watch. It might have a musical attachment. More expensive varieties feature a music box that winds up and plays as the objects move. In this way, baby's sense of hearing is also augmented. He begins to associate cadence of sound with physical movement—a precursor to a sense of rhythm.

Consider a tape recorder placed on a nearby shelf. As the baby adjusts to sleep, quiet music and the slowly moving mobile will nurture gentle rest. And, when baby awakens, there is something interesting to watch that is calming.

When baby is two months old, give or take, put the mobile at the foot of the crib so she can see it easily but where it is out of harm's way. For variety, you might trade mobiles with other parents.

Be sure to remove hanging objects from the infant's grasp when he can sit up and extend his reach because he will pull down a delicate mobile. Instead, you might move it to another part of the room as a decoration. Always check and adjust the mobile's distance from the baby as he grows, especially when he can turn, reach out, and stand.

Mobiles are made by Fisher-Price, Mattel Infant, PlaySkool, and Wimmer-Ferguson. $10–$30.

## 3. Music Boxes and Tape Recorders

Music is important to the sounds your baby hears. Select a music box and locate a tape recorder, as these are good investments for use throughout childhood. Hearing music and listening to stories are great ways for baby to absorb knowledge and sounds, to relax and enjoy auditory stimulation. You can sing songs and your baby will giggle and appreciate your rendition of Madonna, Whitney Houston, Paula Abdul, Linda Ronstadt, Art Garfunkel, or your favorite recording. Sounds of popular or classical music will delight. Put on Beethoven's "Ode to Joy," Rachmaninoff's "Variations on a Theme from Paganini," Mozart's *Eine Kleine Nachtmusik*, Wagner's "Pilgrims' Chorus" from *Tannhäuser*, Bach's "Aria," and, without fail, Tchaikovsky's "The Nutcracker Suite." These offer your offspring early (and, optimally, continuing) exposure to the classics, and a grounding in music appreciation.

## 4. Rattles

Rattles stimulate auditory awareness and hand/eye coordination, and they get the baby's attention. Different rattles make a variety of sounds and many have a calming effect. When a baby is irritated, she will be distracted by the soft shaking sound and turn to it. Be sure to keep your baby's rattles washed and away from heat. You want to be sure whatever comes close to your baby's mouth is clean. You do not want the rattle to be damaged. You do have to keep an eye not only on your child but also on what he plays with.

Different rattles offer different sounds for different occasions. When you change your infant, a rattle will occupy and calm her. Take along several with various sounds when you are away from home, at the pediatrician's, visiting, or traveling. Other rattles will soothe her when she is teething or fussing. By experiment you'll learn which rattles work best. Call the baby's name and shake the rattle gently as you talk or sing to her quietly. Don't overuse it or the baby will lose interest. Rattles provide easy finger exercise and give the baby something easy to grasp.

Some rattles are designed for very young infants; later teething-ring rattles are available for the older child. Rattles may be found in smooth wood; clear, soft plastic; and durable cloth. Some have surprise objects inside to watch for and provide extra visual interest.

> **PLAY POINT:** It is best to get baby adjusted to being in a playpen before she starts crawling or it will not work as effectively later on. In the beginning, she should not be in the playpen for other than a very short time, and only if you need to handle some activity that needs your complete attention. Take her out and engage her in another activity before she starts, or at the earliest signs of, fussing. Set up the playpen in the room where you will be working if at all possible.

Buying a rattle from a company you have researched gives you reasonable assurance that the toy is not defective, will not fall apart, and meets toy-safety standards. Reliable rattles are made by BRIO, Chicco, Fisher-Price, Gerber, Kiddie-Kraft, Learning Curve, Plakie, and Sassy. $1-$8.

## 5. Stuffed Toys

Soft, stuffed-toy animals are collected from the time you send out birth announcements to your offspring's adolescence and beyond. These toys are consistently popular. The baby will probably receive several which can be displayed easily on shelves; don't let them clutter the crib. One is adequate as a stimulating, visual plaything.

Stuffed-toy play grows with the baby. At first "teddy" is strictly decorative, but as the child grows he will find comfort in his soft, plush animal. The connection is soothing. He will want to taste him, grasp him, let him fall down, and throw him. As his ability to grasp, hold, and lift objects develops, so does his attachment to teddy.

Soft toys are also a source of communication. Your baby will begin to make sounds to teddy, just as he makes sounds when you are near. Let the new plush friend "speak" with the baby when you first take the toy to him and he will relate more quickly to it.

Soft animals work well on car trips and are convenient to amuse the baby if he gets cranky. When the toy "talks" about the adventures you both share on the trip—the passing sights, the next stop—time will pass quickly for the contented baby.

Babies fuss for attention, so a combination of parent and soft panda is a treat. If *you* talk with the panda, later on the baby will also. You set the example and your little one will watch you for cues. A great deal of language will be communicated by an imaginative child who talks with his soft toy.

Special plush animals are created just for the infant, so shop carefully. Soft toys which are "baby-proof" are small, cuddly, hypoallergenic, and sturdily washable. And whether the soft animal is a gift from yourself or another, make sure each one is safe: Look for embroidered eyes, not buttons; see that appliquéd noses and ears are well stitched, not glued; check that the plush or terry cloth is good quality and won't fray or shed lint into her mouth. If you want to provide a special gift, invest in a teddy bear or a soft, washable hippopotamus, tiger, elephant, or whatever other animal you will enjoy looking at and playing with. Some of these delightful animals make a sound when turned over. Whatever one you purchase will delight baby.

Soft toys from Applause, Eden, Fisher-Price, GUND, Hugg-A-Planet, Learning Curve, Manhattan Baby, PlaySkool, Russ Berrie, and Steiff are recommended. $5–$30.

# SIX WEEKS TO SIX MONTHS
## Babies Expand Their Play

You will enjoy watching the rapid changes in your infant during this next period. Baby lifts up his head while lying on his stomach and follows movement with increased concentration. He smiles more, makes many new sounds, and watches intently as you move about.

Baby examines her fingers and yours, and puts them into her mouth. She grasps teething rings and swings them about; she'll squeeze animals and experiment with her toes, fingers, and stray objects. Inquisitive babies like to explore everything, so this is a time to be careful about what is left within your baby's grasp.

The six-week-old will watch mobiles for long periods of time and be delighted if objects are changed once in a while. When he fusses for attention, you can distract and amuse him with a single toy.

In the first half year, your baby pays attention to her hands and feet, and shifts attention from her fingers to soft teething rings. She starts differentiating between near and far. She will grasp small objects, the edge of a blanket, or anything that captivates her attention—mom's earring, dad's keys. Watch out for pulls!

Babies now use both hands and want to bring everything to their mouths. Your little one will like toys that can make sounds or movements. He'll love looking at a mirror and be fascinated with the smiling image he sees there making sounds so much like his own, so add (safety) mirror games to your playtimes together. Mirror play, especially with you, will intrigue your baby for many months.

Sit or hold the mirror in front of your baby's face so he can stare at the "other" baby, reach for his image, pat his friend, or even bestow a kiss, especially with your encouragement.

Point to his reflection and say, "I see Duane. Can you see Duane?" Then hold the mirror so both of your faces are visible. "Now I see Daddy, too! Do you see Daddy?" While your baby looks at himself, point to and name the different parts of his face. Or with both of you looking, point to his features, then your own.

Now it is critical to watch what babies are holding or chewing on. If an object can hurt her in any way do not allow it within reach. Her movements will be rapid and she can find trouble in a blink of your eyes.

Your little one will begin to be charmed by games such as peekaboo with familiar persons. She will laugh easily at her new, funny world and react to particular people.

## TOY SUGGESTIONS FOR BABIES IN FIRST SIX MONTHS

### 6. Cloth Blocks

These blocks are made of foam with a variety of coverings and often have pictures on the sides. Some are covered with vinyl and can be easily washed. Cloth blocks are among baby's earliest experiences with shapes. They promote depth perception and visual

## BABY TOYS TO SIX MONTHS

| | | |
|---|---|---|
| 6. Cloth blocks | (C) | tactile stimulus; small-muscle coordination (grasping, spatial awareness) |
| 7. Crib toys and gyms | (AE) | all-senses stimulus; small-muscle coordination |
| 8. Link rings | (A) | tactile stimulus; small-muscle coordination |
| 9. Mirrors | (C) | visual stimulus (eye focusing, self-image perception) |
| 10. Soft balls | (A) | tactile stimulus; small-muscle coordination (grasping, throwing, retrieving) |
| 11. Teethers | (A) | touch, taste, visual, possibly sound stimulus (gum exercise, color/shape perception, rattle sounds) |

sharpness and, together with blocks she'll play with as she grows older, teach concepts of size and direction: up, down, big, little.

Baby enjoys playing with his cloth blocks both with you and by himself. In the beginning he'll just hold them and push them around. Later he'll start trying to stack them. Finally, he'll stack them up, and then make the whole stack tumble down! Why not? It's fun!

Blocks are a classic toy. Like all classic toys, they pave the pathway to discovery. Different types of blocks will be used over the next five years of learning, and then are permuted into elaborate construction shapes.

Choices for blocks include those from Chicco, Cultural Toys, Fisher-Price, Mattel Infant, and PlaySkool. $5–$14.

## 7. Crib Toys and Gyms

As your baby begins to grasp different things, he will seek items to hold, push, and pull. A number of good handheld toys and crib gyms are available and can be used by baby even before he sits up. These toys and activities become more entertaining as he enters the fourth month.

The crib gym is a securely mounted bar with interesting objects safely suspended within reach. As baby lies on her back, the gym will entertain her for long periods of time. Gyms are designed from the simple to the more complicated, and as you compare all of the choices keep in mind what attracts your baby and what you feel she needs.

For the first couple of months a crib toy is not needed. Your baby will not do much more than play with you and react to his immediate environment. As he gets older, simple crib attachments can broaden his attention. He will focus on new shapes; he will reach out, push, make sounds, practice grasping, and use his small muscles.

A variety is recommended. Try to maintain a balance of different types in each of the active, creative, and educational categories and do not overdo with too many things.

As baby grows, the crib gym can graduate to floor play, as you must be sure that nothing stretches across the crib when baby starts to raise himself (as early as five months with some) and might reach it. Dangerous, then!

A number of fine crib toys and crib gyms are produced by Chicco, Fisher-Price, Learning Curve, Manhattan Baby, PlaySkool, and Sassy. $3–$30.

## 8. Link Rings

Link rings are molded pieces of plastic that fit easily together to become a colorful chain with great play value. Whether used across the top of the crib sides when baby is very young or as loose, short segments for baby to handle, they make a colorful attention-getter with a satisfying, soft clatter whether baby is playing in the crib or on a trip. They have added value when they double as teethers.

The links are made of preformed durable plastic in primary colors and allow your young one to pull them apart and put them together easily. They enhance hand/eye coordination and provide a challenge to baby's curious mind, and they are among the most useful toys available for the four- to six-month-old.

Good link rings are made by Chicco, Discovery Toys, Fisher-Price, Galt Toys, International Playthings, and PlaySkool. $5–$10.

## 9. Mirrors

An unbreakable mirror is a device that will absorb baby's attention. It helps her become alert to her eyes, nose, mouth, hair, fingers, and different parts of her body.

It's good for her to see herself; she'll gurgle and talk to that interesting new "playmate" and you can play peekaboo games with her in the mirror. She will become aware that it is her own image she's looking at when she sees the two of you. This is the beginning of consciousness of her own personhood. This is a process of self-discovery and aids in promoting baby's positive feelings about herself.

Mirrors must be unbreakable, with edges completely enclosed. The best place to put one up is inside on the crib's side where baby can be contented to watch and babble with her "companion" while you are busy. Safe mirrors are marketed by Fisher-Price and PlaySkool. $10–$20.

## 10. Soft Balls

Babies love to reach out and try to hold on to objects, and balls become especially interesting to your child at this stage. Baby will throw a small ball and receive it back with delighted squeals. Be sure the ball is light so she can grab and lift it easily, and it also will not hurt her when she bumps herself with a wild toss! Specially designed handles make a large, soft foam ball easier to hold. Look also for see-through balls with a captivating object at which baby can peer.

A soft ball is good for developing small-muscle coordination and gripping, and they are made to fit the baby's hand. The balls should be washable as they will inevitably end up in baby's mouth, and so too must be large enough to avoid any choking danger!

As you give baby the ball you will be able to notice whether he is tending to right- or left-handedness when he reaches for it. Babies are often ambidextrous at this age, however, and preference may be established later. Do not try to force your baby's hand-edness; it is perfectly all right to direct a toy casually toward his right hand, so long as you do not make him uncomfortable if he takes it with his left.

Speak the word for the toy as you offer it to her and while she plays with it. "Ball" is a word she will learn early; it's easy to say. By repeating the word frequently, you'll acquaint her with the connection between the sound and the object.

You will find balls in many sizes, colors, and coverings from which to select. Look for Battat, Chicco, Fisher-Price, PlaySkool, and Small World Toys products. $3.50–$10.

## 11. Teethers

As your baby is teething and continues to suck, she will also need to soothe and exercise her gums. She can do that best with a sturdy and appealing teething ring. Some are made to make a soft, rattle sound. Choose from among plastic, rubber, and wood and be sure your selection is easy for your baby to hold.

For a range of teethers look at Chicco, Fisher-Price, Gerber Learning Curve, PlaySkool, and Sassy. $2–$10.

# SIX MONTHS TO ONE YEAR
## Baby's Rapid Changes

It is a marvelous experience to watch your baby go from lying and sleeping most of the time to being active, alert, and curious. Your baby is now growing quickly, doubling his birth weight and more, and he is acquiring new skills and abilities with great speed. He grasps your hands and lifts his head. He likes to roll over and wriggle about.

Baby will be able to go from lying flat to sitting up by herself. She changes into a baby who has the ability to build, push and pull objects, grasp and loosen objects with increasing decision, and hold on to things.

Her general mobility escalates and some babies, depending on height and weight, may even stand alone and attempt those first steps. Teeth have come in during this period and the teething ring is well-used. You will get some great aerobic bends in during this time: A fun thing for baby is to drop items and watch mommy and daddy pick them up.

Baby's language develops at a rapid rate from the first sounds of "mama" to several words. He is able to identify sounds, look for things, and demand attention. You will also notice that your child may sometimes be shy around strangers, but when he knows a person he will react with great animation. This is also a period when your little one has difficulty separating from his mother.

You now have to pay very close attention to what she wants to put into her mouth (like balloons, small objects) and where she moves herself. As her dexterity increases, your baby will tend to taste and gnaw shapes just from curiosity. This can be dangerous. Watch carefully!

During the six-month to one-year period your baby will begin to engage in games and make imitative sounds. This is the time when it is rewarding to play "finger" and "peekaboo" with him.

He likes toys that make things happen. He is delighted when, as a result of his actions, bells ring or wheels turn. Things that disappear will entrance him, and stacking boxes and reaching for things will hold his attention for longer lengths of time.

From about the age of six months on your baby will resist when you stop his play and will fuss about this profusely. At the same time, now he will listen, fascinated, to mother and father reading words aloud and will love to turn pages (not, of course, necessarily in synch with the reader!). This, with baby snuggled close in your lap, is one of the greatest joys of being a parent or grandparent.

Be sure to "baby-proof" your house, as your baby's curiosity and mobility can expose her to some objects which are breakable or hazardous. Get down on the floor and see your living space from your curious baby's viewpoint. Everything looks like fun. Make sure everything is safe. Covers on plugs, gates across stairs. Nothing easy to pull down. No loose objects that can break. Nothing that can be of danger to your baby. Be alert!

## TOY SUGGESTIONS FOR BABIES SIX MONTHS TO ONE YEAR

### 12. Assorted Kitchen Items

"Can my child use simple objects like kitchen utensils?" many parents ask. I always say, "Yes!" Kitchen items are handy and relatively inexpensive. Such items were used by moms for generations to keep baby amused while mom was tending the fire, preparing family meals, and doing other household tasks. Today there are many quality wood and plastic kitchen products that are perfect for babies at this age and throughout early childhood. Somehow, when all else fails, these common items seem to do the trick with a curious or fretting baby. The introduction of something new will get your baby's attention and be of interest.

You might consider buying several six- or nine-inch plastic bowls, plastic measuring cups, and a few sponges just for your

## NEW TOYS, MORE SKILLS

| | | |
|---|---|---|
| 12. Assorted kitchen items | (A) | visual, tactile; small-muscle coordination |
| 13. Flutter balls | (A) | visual, tactile; flexing |
| 14. Large puzzles | (E) | visual, tactile; space and form perception |
| 15. Nesting blocks | (A) | visual, tactile; motor skills |
| 16. Push-pull toys | (A) | visual, tactile, auditory; large-muscle development; sound differentiation |
| 17. Shape-sorting boxes | (E) | visual, tactile; shape and form perception |
| 18. Soft dolls | (C) | visual, tactile, olfactory; language and emotional development |
| 19. Stacking towers | (E) | visual, tactile; small-muscle coordination |

baby to play with. These, plus lightweight pots and pans and other simple household items, can ignite your baby's imagination throughout the next two years. No glass, pottery, china, or sharp utensils, of course, may be part of baby's collection. Decide which items you want for baby and keep them separate and clean in a sturdy plastic tub. Your baby will find these toys delightful and will want to play with them often.

Rubbermaid and Tupperware are good choices for kitchen playthings. $5–$10.

## 13. Flutter Balls

These are large clear plastic balls with a butterfly, bee, or other small, colorful object inside that moves about. The interior shape captures the baby's attention and helps him learn to focus. He can push the globe about on surfaces with his hands or feet, and the figure inside turns and flutters about in reaction.

Fisher-Price offers one, as does PlaySkool. $10.

## 14. Large Puzzles

Some excellent picture puzzles are made with only a few large pieces (three to five) cut into easy shapes that fit together. Babies enjoy putting pieces down together and sometimes even (usually at random) make them fit, especially if lines are drawn on the board for clues as to where to put each one.

This is the kind of toy where parents might demonstrate once or twice but should *not* insist baby "keep within the black lines." At this stage, coordination is still developing and "fits" of the pieces will often be accidental. Let your little one play happily and unconstrainedly with them; "fitting" the forms together will come when he's ready.

The puzzles may be wooden, plastic, or of durable sponge material. Some have knobs for easier grasp.

Primary-level jigsaw puzzles are available through Age Appropriate Puzzles, Anatex, Fisher-Price, Galt Toys, Lauri, PlaySkool, and TC Timber. $5–$10.

## 15. Nesting Blocks

A gratifying activity for baby now is learning to stack and place things inside each other. The shaped and hollowed nesting blocks are designed for her to put the plastic cups inside each other and see how they fit. They provide good practice in hand/eye coordination.

Baby will use these hollow blocks for a long time. Later, she will fill them with sand, water, or even other toys, and invent new kinds of filling and emptying activities.

BRIO, Fisher-Price, Galt Toys, and PlaySkool are possible choices. $5–$10.

## 16. Push-Pull Toys

As your baby begins to move about more, he enjoys pushing and pulling objects that move along the floor. You can begin with a push-pull toy he can use from a sitting position. These push-pull toys are a great way for baby to announce his efforts, and he relishes the response of others to this activity. Talk with him about it as he moves about. He will imitate a train, a car, or a plane as he moves. You will be amazed at what he has picked up from his travels with you in the real world.

Occasionally this toy can get to your ears after a while. Be prepared and be patient!

BRIO, Fisher-Price, and PlaySkool offer good choices. $10–$20.

## 17. Shape-Sorting Boxes

With this plaything, geometric shapes fit through openings of like shapes cut out of a large square box. Your baby finds it fascinating to put the shapes through the holes and when she succeeds they make a satisfying sound as she drops them. This is the original "pushing a square peg into a round hole" activity and when baby cannot make *that* work, she learns, it is hoped, not to force things that don't fit!

The shape-sorting box is another toy that may be difficult for some babies at first, so don't worry if your child is not initially interested. Make the toy available to intrigue her and for her to experiment with, and watch what happens four to six weeks later.

Shape-sorting boxes are offered by Fisher-Price, Holgate, Mattel, PlaySkool, and TC Timber. $10–$20.

## 18. Soft Dolls

Manufacturers now produce dolls that are soft, simple, washable, and cuddly. They have no buttons to come loose. The soft fabric bodies have faces sewn on. The seams are tight; the stuffing is made of quality, washable materials. These dolls are perfect for six-month- to one-year-old babies. Talk to the baby while playing with the doll. They will find it funny and will babble to the doll also. Baby takes clues about play from you.

Choose dolls from those by BRIO, Fisher-Price, Hugg-A-Planet, Manhattan Baby, and PlaySkool. $5–$10.

## 19. Stacking Towers

Perception of colors, shapes, sizes, and quantities is enhanced by stacking towers. Colored doughnut-shaped rings made of strong molded plastic or wood are stacked loosely on a dowel. You will find this a toy that grows with the child, and he will perform increasingly complex and imaginative tasks with it as he matures.

Stacking towers are offered by Chicco, Fisher-Price, and PlaySkool $5–$15.

---

## DR. TOY'S TIPS FOR KEEPING TOYS SAFE & CLEAN

Follow these steps for washable, colorfast toys:

1. Wash toys with hot, soapy water (use rubber gloves, if necessary, to allow the hottest tap water). Rinse thoroughly.
2. Soak toys in a solution of 3/4 cup Clorox household bleach dissolved in 1 gallon of water. (This may fade some plastics and even some "colorfast" fabrics. Watch labels for warnings against chlorine and consider a recommended substitute, bearing in mind that the chlorine solution is a basic germ-killer.)
3. Let stand five minutes.
4. Rinse chlorine solution out thoroughly.
5. Dry: air dry or dry by hand with a fresh, clean towel. Do *not* use a dryer unless the label okays it.

## ▶ SUMMARY

# Baby's Play Activities in the First Year

The following are specific skills your baby develops with the kinds of toys best suited for these skills. Your child:

- *Focuses on items* like mobiles.
- *Heightens his senses* with playthings like soft toys, balls, or puppets.
- *Is fascinated and extends attention span* with responses from things that "act back" like squeak toys, link chains, and bath toys that make a lovely splash.
- *Learns self-awareness/self-confidence* with mirrors.
- *Grows in emotional attachments* by holding soft toys and dolls.
- *Responds to his own physical needs* with teething rings, push-pull toys, or crib gyms.
- *Discovers and develops his ability to reach out and control* with grasping toys.
- *Differentiates and appreciates sounds* through musical tapes and CDs.
- *Increases physical dexterity* with empty boxes, nesting blocks, wooden spoons, and water play.
- *Sharpens visual skills* with soft washable books; marking paper with large, nontoxic crayons; and manipulating large-piece puzzles.

## Physical, Mental, and Emotional Developmental Milestones During Baby's First Six Months

- Gains motor control: can reach and grasp.
- Discovers feet: brings feet to mouth.

- Begins sitting with support.
- Plays supported in a sitting position.
- Large-muscle play includes rolling, scooting, rocking, bouncing.
- Follows objects visually. Gazes toward moving objects.
- Learns where sounds come from; turns to sounds.
- Responds to rhythm, music, singing.
- Explores hands, feet, and mouth.
- Enjoys responses: his own, his playthings', people's.
- Recognizes familiar people and can separate them.
- Aware of strangers.
- Imitates simple movements.
- Interested in people's faces and voices.
- Smiles at faces, voices, mirror image.
- Wants attention and contact with others.
- Makes sounds in response to social contact.
- Reacts to emotional tones.
- Makes various sounds and laughs.
- Listens and imitates.

**PLAY POINTS** Baby needs warm, nurturing play experiences from everyone in the family. Remember to talk, sing, and have fun. Provide soft stimulation from music, colors, voice, and rocking. Toys should be used for short periods of time. The parent is the baby's biggest toy—that relationship is the most important bond.

Baby's toys should be a combination of:

- Bright, primary nontoxic colors.
- Clear, simple, design.
- High contrast of shape, colors, sizes.
- Attractive patterns.
- Ability to be hung, to move or sway, to make an attractive sound.
- Capacity for generating baby's responses easily.
- Capability that encourages looking, listening, sucking, grasping, or fingering and sustains a child's interest.

## Physical, Mental, and Emotional Development Markers During Baby's Second Six Months

- Likes to have a teddy or soft doll to hold and cuddle.
- Enjoys a larger selection of toys.
- Wants to hold items that make sounds.
- Needs gradually more complex challenges to gain motor control.
- Drawn to hold, let go, and retrieve small objects.
- Plays with busy box and engages in more complicated activities.
- Stacks and arranges blocks.
- Grabs objects in either hand.
- Enjoys give and take of balls; moves toward them.
- Marks up paper with crayons.
- Rolls over from front to back.
- Can lift herself to sitting from lying down.
- Can sit for a short time unsupported.
- Rocks from side to side, sitting, later on all fours.
- Reaches for toys.
- Likes to babble; will listen for reply (be sure to babble back, talk, sing, and respond to him).
- Raises voice to get attention.
- Understands certain words by the end of the first year; responds to those frequently heard.
- Begins to use her own words.
- Focuses on objects, looks toward something that has been dropped.
- Picks up objects.
- Will look for a toy that has gone out of sight.
- Pays attention to things close by and up to ten feet away.
- Likes to fill empty containers.
- Makes noise: bangs on surfaces, shakes objects that make sounds.
- Imitates tones others make.

- Some babies begin to pull themselves up by holding on to furniture.
- Many babies can "walk" while their hands are held.
- Likes peekaboo and clapping games.

## Safety

Check carefully for overall safety, ease and limits of use, and value of equipment purchases including:

- bike seat
- carrier
- cradle
- crib
- helmet
- jumper
- portable seat for car
- safety gate
- stroller
- swing

# THREE

# Toddler

## THE ONE- TO THREE-YEAR-OLD

Sally eagerly bought many toys for her toddler that appealed to her. But when she got home and gave them to Ryan, he just looked at them with disinterest and turned away to play with the cat. Sally felt irritated and uncertain about what to do, and we talked about it. She wanted to play with him but the situation overwhelmed her. I suggested some books about child development and through her reading Sally learned about Ryan in ways that helped her understand and play with him better. She became acquainted with her child's natural interests and energy cycles, learned to introduce toys one at a time, and mastered the art of being more patient with Ryan and with herself. In other words, Sally learned to be Ryan's most effective Play Tutor. She even found a picture book about cats that got his interest.

Sally and her husband, Bob, devised an easy storage area for Ryan's toys, and thus prevented his play space from getting cluttered (which can be frustrating when a child wants to explore an open area). When Sally realized that Ryan wasn't rejecting her, she was able to see that he was just more fascinated with a live creature—their cat and its responses—than with the armful of lovely toys she brought him that, by their very number and variety, had put his senses into overload.

Bob and Sally diagnosed Ryan's level in his natural growth pattern and played with him more, talking and piquing his interest and discovering and meeting his needs. For example, when he wanted a quiet activity, they showed him a puzzle. When Ryan saw how the pieces fit together he was so delighted he emptied the frame and did the puzzle again and again.

We discussed the changes in the average child at the age of one year: He has grown about half again his birth length and tripled his birth weight. The toddler has gained control of head, body, arms, and legs, and his skills have increased. At this time he is crawling rapidly and sometimes walking and will easily climb on furniture.

## Passing the First Birthday

At the beginning of her second year, your baby's attention span is not great. A toddler is mostly interested in watching, exploring, moving, and delights in knocking things over to see reactions— not just what happens to what she pushed, but what happens to mommy and daddy when they see the cup of milk pooling on the shiny floor.

The toddler comes to learn about cause and effect (hit a mallet and a peg falls into the hole; or push a button, music plays and a doll dances; turn a handle and a jack-in-the-box pops up and bounces).

Interesting new sounds come from your growing baby now, and he creates words like "bye, ma ma, da da, dat." His under-standing of words has expanded as he picks up your tone of voice and your meaning, and he is aware of your feelings. Playing games with you is a favorite pastime. Patty-cake, peekaboo, clapping to music are new entries to his repertoire. People and animals fascinate, and he loves to make sounds and act silly. He wants to laugh, giggle, and be surprised. Parents fascinate the toddler, and they will remain in this enviable position for the first three years of his life—and be his best playmates for many more. Adults often enjoy being silly with little children, and if a grown-up allows himself to talk and behave in funny ways his child will give him total and appreciative attention.

The toddler is very much attached to the people closest to her. Relationships formed during the earliest months are basic to her emotional progress, and the connection and friendship between toddler and parent allows her to move into the larger world of friends and other players. Parents who play and respond to their children are more important to their offspring's health and well-being than any toy.

Now your toddler will act out his feelings, fantasies, and experiences during play. Understanding your child's moods helps a lot. Some days your child will be stubborn and fussy, sometimes quiet, sometimes very active, sometimes very intent on examining objects closely. And sometimes a child shows no interest whatever. You can see moods reflected in the activities he selects. Give him his freedom to express these moods, and make whatever adaptations to his environment they require (whether it is the kind of toy he plays with, a snack, or a nap). Time has no importance to him and he will be absorbed in the activity of the moment: pouring water, rolling a ball, or watching a spinning pinwheel.

The age at which a child pulls herself up to sitting, hauls herself to a stand while supported, and walks about holding on to the hands of others is a highly individual thing and depends a great deal on her size and weight. Some babies begin this process as early as halfway into their first year; others won't begin it until well after their first birthday. *When* your baby starts to sit, crawl, stand, and toddle, whether very early or very late, should not be a cause for alarm—as your pediatrician will tell you. Only she can and should decide if baby's development deserves additional attention.

Remember, you are a "Tutor," not a "trainer."

Do not force your little one to walk before he is ready or put too much weight on his legs before the bones are sufficiently strong. This causes problems later.

## ACTIVITIES TYPICAL OF THE TODDLER

Your toddler usually . . .

- Loves playing with items like dustpans, brooms, plastic dishes, pots/pans, and cups.
- Imitates the actions of others: tries drinking from a cup and talking on a telephone. He will hammer with a mallet on wooden pegs after seeing daddy tap a pipe on an ashtray or mommy rap a tight jar cap to loosen it.
- Sees physical differences between herself and others.
- Likes to experiment for reactions. She is drawn to objects that bounce, make noise, light up, or change colors.
- Delights in fitting things together and stacking blocks, toys, and cups. Toddlers like to assemble and disassemble—all the while learning sizes, shapes, colors, weight, and sequencing.
- Can enjoy quiet play, picture books, and looking at things. Talking about pictures, pointing to them, and learning new words intrigue him.
- Likes to listen to music and imitate the sounds of records and tapes. She tries to understand your words.
- When he recognizes his favorite toys or animals in books, he will show his excitement.
- If you have taken your baby with you on errands from her early months, she will love to travel and to go different places.
- Likes: building things, creating art, digging in sand, looking at and pasting pictures, playing with animals, squeezing objects, taking walks and going on rides, throwing things, and water play.

As your baby's second year begins, her world is opening up. She has a natural curiosity and is bound to get into things. If not carefully supervised, she can be badly injured. For example, the toddler will open bottles or boxes to touch or taste. Anything that is potentially dangerous must be placed in locked cabinets and well out of reach.

We need to strike a balance between giving our kids protection and allowing them freedom of self-discovery. Children have accidents just as we do. We wish we could always protect them so nothing serious ever happens to them, and with planning and preparation, most accidents can be avoided.

## Playing with Other Children

This is the time for parents to connect with play groups and with each other, so that their children can socialize. The youngsters will, at first, engage in parallel play, that is, solo play alongside other children. Sometimes they will do the same activity (like sandbox bulldozing and landfill), but at their own pace. However, they do learn new ways to play from each other.

If you notice that your child is shy with people or other children, or seems to be withdrawn, first encourage him to play with puppets and human figures: simple soft dolls or well-crafted action mannequins. Introduce other children casually. Slowly, your child will play with one child, then another. It won't always go smoothly, but it will be a good learning experience.

> **PLAY POINT:**
>
> Always take along interesting small toys for your toddler to play with when traveling. He will be happier and so will you. Create a Play Bag for your child that is filled with things he will find fun. Also remember to talk about the trip along the way even if it's only to the grocery store. These are the best times to share communication, as your child likes to travel and to learn along the way. You may also want to sing.

Soon she will follow or lead another youngster, each one eager to get responses from the other. Your toddler will begin to enjoy contact with other playmates, although she or the other child will usually be possessive of her own toys, and will fuss if another child grabs one.

If your child is aggressive and pulls things away from other children, try to teach him understanding, sharing, and cooperative play but, again, don't force a child to "share." There's no surer way to teach him slyness in protecting what is his. Distraction might work—substituting another favorite to help him choose to share, or perhaps, if the other child is comfortable about it, even a temporary trade. If you can keep the experience cheerful and pleasing, do it. Otherwise, wait for a future stage of development to try again.

Toddlers get into fights easily, but these are soon forgotten. Just be sure that when several children are together there are sufficient objects to play with both individually and sharing. And distraction, not scolding (especially in front of peers), is the golden word.

## The Home-Toy Factory . . .

Each year toys for toddlers are improved and refined and buying them is fun. When your little one was an infant you may have created toys for her. Don't stop now! You can still make items which will teach skills such as hand/eye coordination, creativity, and physical development, and will also give your child something of special value no store-bought item can provide. So, back to the pattern books and this time, let her "help." Involve her with the creation. Encourage her to tell you what she wants in her new toy. Imagine the delight for you both, the enrichment, the stimulation, the bonding you can share.

As for the baby who has just passed his first birthday, organize his playthings into the categories that follow.

**A** CTIVE   (promotes hand/eye coordination, muscle tone, strength)
**C** REATIVE          (encourages spontaneity, self-expression)
**E** DUCATIONAL          (challenges thinking, mental growth)

## TOY SUGGESTIONS FOR TODDLERS ONE TO TWO YEARS OLD

|     |                      |     |
| --- | -------------------- | --- |
| 1.  | Art supplies         | (C) |
| 2.  | Balls                | (A) |
| 3.  | Bath toys            | (A) |
| 4.  | Blocks               | (A) |
| 5.  | Books                | (E) |
| 6.  | Dolls                | (C) |
| 7.  | Pails and shovels    | (A) |
| 8.  | Pounding sets        | (A) |
| 9.  | Push-pull toys       | (A) |
| 10. | Puzzles              | (E) |
| 11. | Ride-on toys         | (A) |
| 12. | Ring stacks          | (E) |
| 13. | Shape-sorting boxes  | (E) |
| 14. | Stuffed animals      | (C) |
| 15. | Surprise boxes       | (E) |

## 1. Art Supplies

Creativity begins early and, if nurtured, becomes an intrinsic part of your child's experiences. Art is a re-creation of what is seen or thought as filtered through the artist's perceptions. Even with fine art's more representational painters, what is produced carries the artist's distinctive spin. Children have their own unique way of seeing and feeling, and when they create a picture, don't ask, "What is it?" when you cannot figure out what they have drawn. Instead ask, "Can you tell me about your picture?" If you respond in a positive way, the child will feel encouraged and happily create more new pictures and art objects. Their work can be done with crayons, finger paints, clay, or cut-and-paste collages. Coloring books, fat crayons, or Magic Markers may also be included.

You can find art supplies especially for children according to age at toy, educational specialty, or stationery stores. You may want to paint or color along with your child and he will enjoy your company once in a while. Don't worry if you haven't painted or drawn for years; vivid memories will come back once you have a crayon in your hand. You may want to obtain a drawing board (with one or two surfaces—blackboard or cork is often found on the second side) and a variety of paper and other supplies. Don't forgt to display the artwork and save some samples with the dates. They will be treasured.

Art supplies are made by ALEX, Battat, BEKA, Binney & Smith, Color Creations, Colorforms, and Galt. $1–$75.

## 2. Balls

One of the classic toys, a ball is a universal everyone can play with and which engages your toddler with siblings and friends. Balls offer a spectrum of sizes, colors, and activities. Rolling them, bouncing them, throwing them, and catching them, all encourage coordination and dexterity.

Be cautious about balls in the house and don't hesitate to establish ground rules from the start. A toddler will accept a rule and it becomes so thoroughly ingrained that when he is junior-high-school age—the great rebellious years—the habit will be formed already and stands a good chance of holding.

Plush, soft, light balls are less likely to cause damage indoors. Hard rubber or beach balls are outdoor toys.

Since balls come in all sizes, indulge in a variety: tennis balls, rubber balls, beach balls, fabric, sponge, and light hollow balls. You and your toddler can throw a ball out-of-doors or roll it back and forth gently inside.

As a rainy-day indoor activity, you might make a hoop from a large wastebasket and let your toddler throw a soft ball into it (and around, behind, and above it!). Consider creating a customized ball, fabric clutch or textured, from sewing remnants that baby helps choose.

Dare we say it? Do have a ball. . . .

Varied balls are offered by Battat, Hugg-A-Planet, Oddzon, and PlaySkool. $1–$8.

## 3. Bath Toys

Bath times become happy times with a few water-safe playthings, but avoid more than a toy or two for each bath. Balls, rubber animals (such as the immortal yellow "Rubber Ducky"), and other floating toys like simple plastic boats are ideal for the toddler. Manufacturers have been rather ingenious in this area and have created a good variety.

If you want to indulge in one of the activity boxes for the tub wall, it will keep your child busy pouring water and making wheels turn. It's a good idea to "rotate" the activity box: take it out for a while, store it, and then put it back. Children get bored if something is around all the time. Washcloth puppets make an added surprise and are good for sneaking in a thorough cleanup.

Bath toys are made by Fisher-Price, Mattel, and PlaySkool. $3–$12.

## 4. Blocks

Throughout childhood, children find hundreds of uses for blocks, which offer enormous flexibility and generate creativity. The younger child will build structures and knock them over. Later she will create tunnels, carports, airports, farms, and houses. Blocks are basic in most nursery schools and child-care programs and children play with them from the toddler stage through kindergarten and later.

A young professor of English, who had completed two novels, told me that blocks were his all-time favorite toys. He could use his imagination to the utmost when playing with them, and he felt they had a special influence on developing his own creative process. Many other people have agreed this was true in their lives.

Start with small blocks—wooden, cardboard, or sponge—that are easy for the one-year-old to grasp. Look for blocks with colorful alphabet letters and pictures. At first the toddler will make small stacks, but as she learns and grows she will start creating more elaborate structures.

As your little one approaches two or two and a half, you will want to give him larger blocks: wood, cardboard, and foam are good materials that vary in weight and texture.

Building blocks are another activity where you and your child can play together—just get down on the floor with her and she will be very pleased with you!

Blocks are made by BRIO, Community Playthings, Galt Toys (soft and hard blocks), Holgate, KAPLA, Mattel, Pappa Geppeto's, PlaySkool, TC Timber, and Uncle Goose. $7–$25.

## 5. Books

*Richer than I you will never be*
*For I had a mother who read to me.*

Books may be the single most consequential part of playtime for children, but they are often forgotten, perhaps, because one seldom thinks of them as "toys." Yet their entertainment value (when used appropriately) cannot be surpassed, and they are essential throughout a child's development. If you want your child to be a reader then read to him.

The very first picture books—of washable cloth or material that is chewable, pull- and tear-proof, and otherwise indestructible—will have large colorful alphabet letters, animals, and big pictures. There is something about a book that grabs a baby's attention long before she associates "story!" with it. (Gosh, Mommy, see those pages flip back and forth! Look at all the colors and shapes on them! Um-mm. Tastes good, too!)

Children pull books out over and over again, especially if you read aloud to them. Talk *about* the stories, too. You'll soon find your toddler "reading" to his puppets or stuffed animals.Consider purchasing books that match favorite dolls or toys, such as Paddington or Pooh bear or Raggedy Ann, and let him hear stories while playing with the story's character.

Publishers for young children include Dutton, Golden Books, Grosset & Dunlap, Harcourt Brace, Macmillan, Morrow, Price-Stern-Sloan, Random House, Sierra Club Books, and Viking. $1–$6.

## 6. Dolls

From the time your child is a baby until he is a teenager, dolls will be central to his play. Soft and cuddly dolls are the first kind to acquire. As your young one gets older, add more variety. Your child will hold, cuddle, talk, and play endlessly with these important friends. Toddlers like to wash dolly in and out of the bathtub.

From dolls girls (and boys) learn to socialize, take care of one another, and release emotions. Dolls promote creative play between children at different stages.

Accessories accompany many dolls, including clothing, beds, carriages, play sets, and other articles. Shop carefully for these as you can easily overdo it. Try not to acquire too many for the toddler and keep the ones you do buy simple. Keeping things simple is always best. Once your little girl is walking easily, she will like a sturdy doll carriage for outdoor play.

Putting "dolly" to bed when the child is ready for bedtime assists in that ritual, and helps both your tired toddler and tired you to settle down more smoothly.

Dolls are created by Corolle, Effanbee, Fisher-Price, Hasbro, Irwin, Mattel, and PlaySkool. $5–$30.

## 7. Pails and Shovels

With all of the new toys available, old favorites are sometimes forgotten. But basic toys are important because they lose neither style nor value. The child needs quiet time to dig and play in dirt, sand, or water. A pail enables the child to carry this important stuff from place to place. The shovel gives him the tool to load or unload the cargo.

Establish an area in your yard for free-form play. If you do not have a space at home, create time for this activity at the park or in a clean sandbox. Give your youngster an area where he can make a mess safely and not be scolded. Digging and getting dirty is serious fun and this is a natural, constructive part of childhood. If your little guy is allowed to work out this form of play naturally in the garden or in an outdoor space, he will feel a lot better and play indoors later without fussing.

Spades and buckets are among the least expensive toys you can buy. They teach your toddler tangible skills: a sense of weight and balance, the transfer of objects, and a concept of space and volume. An appreciation of natural things is part of the value of outdoor messy play.

Manufacturers for these items are Battat, International Playthings, and Small World Toys. $2–$6.

## 8. Pounding Sets

Toddlers delight in seeing the results of their actions and in doing something that gets a response. What better fun is there than knocking a peg through a hole with a hammer? This toy also has the advantage of developing hand/eye coordination, and allows your toddler to ventilate feelings in an acceptable way. Toddlers find noise most satisfying and pounding keeps your toddler busy for a long time.

You probably can endure only so much thudding, so make this an outdoor activity for sanity's sake (yours).

These toys are made with extra strength and are designed to withstand the pounding. In fact, you may want to try it also. Your child will be entranced as you pound away, and you'll be amazed at how good it feels sometimes!

If your baby does not like to hammer when she first receives the set, put it away and bring it out later for a birthday or other special occasion. She will find her own time when it is right for her.

Be patient and be careful she does not use the hammer on anything breakable. Parents must, of course, teach the proper use of any tools or toys.

Pounding sets are made by BRIO, Fisher-Price, Galt Toys, and PlaySkool. $5–$12.

## 9. Push-Pull Toys

The growing toddler enjoys pushing and pulling objects as he takes his earliest (sure) steps. Animals on a platform base attached to a string and equipped with wheels are a good example. Many do more than just roll along, and heads may bob, wings flutter, legs pump, often accompanied by delicious squawks, clacks, rumbles, and squeaks. Your little one will grip the end of the string and learn to make the object move, discovering the results of her actions and obtaining a response from the toy.

A variation of the pull object on a string is the wooden rod attached to a clear ball that's filled with small balls or figures. The rod toys make noise when pulled or pushed as the balls flip around while making sounds. Your toddler will work this toy gleefully.

When you shop for push-pull toys, be sure the plastic is non-breakable, and that the balls or objects inside are not so small as to be swallowed in the unlikely event they come away from the outer globe. Check that all the parts are firmly secured and do not have segments that can break off. Refer to pages 18–19 for safety pointers on toy selection. Always think safety before giving your child any toy!

As for the racket, look on the bright side. These toys are great sentinels as your youngster explores. The minute you hear silence—check!

Push-pull toys are available from BRIO, Fisher-Price, Galt Toys, Hasbro, and PlaySkool. $7–$20.

## 10. Puzzles

Many children are intrigued by puzzles, from the first one made up of four or five pieces, through complicated jigsaw puzzles later on. When you shop for puzzles, be sure they are easy to follow. The first puzzle for your toddler should be one that is a whole picture that she can lift out smoothly and replace. Some puzzles have the picture underneath the removable pieces.

Puzzles like these provide practice in small muscle control and hand/eye coordination.

Good puzzles are made of wood or cardboard and have labels that assure you of nontoxic colors. Ones with knobs on the pieces are useful for children with special needs.

Your toddler will have puzzle experiences in child care or nursery school. You might want to swap with other parents to offer more variety for your children.

Puzzles are made by BRIO, Colorforms, Fisher-Price, Galt Toys, Lauri, and PlaySkool. $3–$10.

## 11. Ride-on Toys

Her first ride on a trike is a thrill for your little one—and for you! Make sure the one you select is sturdy and well balanced, and is the correct size for your youngster.

Other ride-on/in toys can be introduced earlier than a tricycle. Many small ones love to rock and there are a number of these kinds to choose from, but the true, classic rocking horse should wait until your youngster is a little older; otherwise, be prepared to hold him securely all the while he's riding.

A hobbyhorse on a pole is great fun as your toddler begins to walk and move around, although she'll grow beyond it more quickly than some other selections. For this reason, consider making one from an old broom, turned upside down, with a horse-head hood over the bristles made of felt (no hemming) with securely glued-on features or even a brown-paper grocery bag tied onto the broom at the "neck." The hobbyhorse has been a classic toy literally for several centuries and makes an ideal introduction to the ride-ons to come.

At about the age of one year, your child will be eager to mount a ride-on toy and move in or with it. If you have neighbors living below you, be sensitive to noise and add carpeting to muffle the sounds.

Consider a train that can be ridden on or in, a truck, or a large, friendly animal for baby to sit inside. If a storage area is included in the design, the child can pack items to take along on the "trip." Even better, you can teach him to pick up cargo for storage (i.e., gather toys and put them away!). If the wheeled rider has a horn or bell and makes noises, so much the better.

It may be well to make shopping for the ride-on toy a shared activity with your child to assure his interest and a good fit. Allow for his fast growth but not so much that riding immediately is inadvisable (i.e., feet unable to reach the floor, potentially falling through the seat, pedals too advanced for present play).

This is a toy that can be passed on to siblings or the children of friends, so obtain a sturdy one to last through the active wear and tear of daily play.

Ride-on toys are available from Fisher-Price, Little Tikes, PlaySkool, and Radio Flyer. $10–$30.

## 12. Ring Stacks

A base is topped by a "cone" of four to six colored rings, graduated in size and removable, fitted over each other to form a rainbow of colors. They're held in place by a vertical dowel centered upright on the base.

The rings teach color, can be used as teethers, and can be moved around by your child. She will pull the rings on and off the stack, rearrange them, then dump them and start over.

Several versions exist that are made of wood and are very durable. When using it, children gain skill in hand/eye coordination, perceiving shapes and colors, sensing their relationships, and learning numbers.

Ring stacks are made by BRIO and Fisher-Price. $4–$8.

## 13. Shape-Sorting Boxes

The shape-sorting box is a toy that developed through the work of Maria Montessori and is based on her observation that children enjoy fitting objects into similarly shaped receptacles.

By matching the shape of the piece to the shape of the aperture on the box, your child discriminates between different shapes, coordinates what he sees to what he feels, gains finger control, and hones trial-and-error problem-solving skills.

Introduce her to one shape at a time in the beginning. Don't force her and please don't show impatience or scold when she tries to push the proverbial square peg into a round hole. Let her discover the answers by watching you and trying by herself. She begins now to absorb information by trial and error, a fundamental, inductive learning process in which she must build skills.

This is an excellent toy! It is educational, holds a child's interest for a long time, is easily learned, and is fun.

The shape-sorting box is available from BRIO, Chicco, Fisher-Price, and Galt Toys. $10–$15.

## 14. Stuffed Animals

These and other soft toys please your tired child, provide cuddly affection, and offer a transition to distract him when mommy and daddy must be elsewhere. A fussy child soon quiets down when a favorite teddy bear is offered. Stuffed animals made of good quality plush, carefully stuffed, and subjected to a thorough testing for safety are widely available. You can be confident about most stuffed animals, but do check labels closely. There are many types to choose from, but don't overdo them, as clutter only confuses the toddler.

Because they make endearing gifts, you may receive quite a number of them—and succumb to a few extra yourself! Put most of them away in a closet until the child is ready for a fresh one. Rotating toys is a good idea; they lose their appeal with too much exposure.

If your youngster is allergic to stuffed animals, one that is leather-covered or made from terry cloth might be a good substitute.

Stuffed animals are made by Applause, Dakin, Fisher-Price, North American Bear Company, and PlaySkool. $5–$25.

## 15. Surprise Boxes

Here is an ingenious toy that allows your child to play with switches and levers (pull, push, and/or turn) that make a door open so that a figure pops up similar to a jack-in- the-box. The fun of this toy is that it allows your youngster to see the immediate results of his actions. He responds and laughs at the toy's reactions, as he manipulates the switches.

Surprise boxes are available from Chicco, Fisher-Price, Galt Toys, and PlaySkool. $10–$15.

ADDITIONAL RECOMMENDATIONS FOR THIS AGE GROUP:

- ❏ Pound a Round (for dexterity and coordination).
- ❏ Stack and Bolt (for finger dexterity and coordination).
- ❏ Threading cubes (teaches sorting, stacking, threading).

# FROM THE SECOND TO THE THIRD BIRTHDAY

By the time the child is two, she is mobile, curious, active, and into everything. She is intensely interested in her surroundings, is acquiring knowledge rapidly, and she's excited about exploring the great unknown (which covers just about everything). She has many, many questions. The twos, like the teens, require, on your part, extraordinarily loving patience, gentle firmness, and consistency.

By the age of two and a half, a child pays more attention to the function of his toys. At the end of his second year, his imagination and attempts at make-believe have become significant in his play. He prefers action figures and dolls, wagons, stuffed animals, and trucks. Later, he will want toys that are like the things he encounters every day, realistic with workable parts and pieces.

## TOY SUGGESTIONS FOR TODDLERS TWO TO THREE YEARS OLD

| | | |
|---|---|---|
| 16. | Blackboard and chalk | (C) |
| 17. | Bubble pipes | (A) |
| 18. | Household objects | (A) |
| 19. | Jacks-in-the-box | (A) |
| 20. | Musical instruments and boxes | (C) |
| 21. | Peg-boards | (E) |
| 22. | Play figures | (C) |
| 23. | Puppets | (C) |
| 24. | Telephones | (C) |
| 25. | Tops | (A) |
| 26. | Transportation toys | (AC) |
| 27. | Wagons | (A) |
| 28. | Wooden beads | (E) |

Toddlers need to participate in many activities with proper supervision. Jean Piaget, the Swiss psychologist, said that a child's intellectual growth depends on his dealing in an active way with objects and people. The toddler learns about life through his environment and through a great deal of social and imaginative play.

Your little one will perform roles pretending she's persons familiar to her (mother, father, doctor, etc.) and playact each character's activities. She'll delight in making up new characters, so create "prop boxes" containing costumes, hats, shoes, bags, fabrics, and other playacting things for her. Such role-playing continues throughout the first five years and beyond, and defines for the child her own identity and an empathy for others.

## 16. Blackboard and Chalk

Although the chalkboard is more suited to the child in his third year or to one who can comprehend on a bit more complex level, it is nonetheless a longtime favorite. Versatile, it offers the younger child a chance to draw pictures over and over again, and the older child a place to experiment and keep his best results for a while.

> **PLAY POINT** Other toys your child has played with earlier, such as bath toys, blocks, books, dolls, stuffed animals, etc., are still interesting and worthwhile. Don't take them away! (She probably would fuss about her favorites if you did.)

More than one medium can be used on the blackboard: white and colored chalks (white is easiest to erase) and water paints that go on with a brush (not as easily removed). However, wax crayons or markers should never be used on a blackboard; they'll ruin the surface. Learning to use things as they are meant to be used is a hard—but necessary—lesson.

There are children who will think of a blackboard as they would paper and want to use crayons on it. To teach your little one not to do this may not be possible (depending on her age and spiritedness), but one technique that may work is to demonstrate on a small, inexpensive, handheld board how chalk and water paints will not work if wax crayons have spoiled the surface.

Keep crayon and paper separate, but available. Provide a simple cover for the chalkboard (an old towel? a worn-out baby blanket?) and make a game of covering the board when there are grinchy crayons near by.

I ruined at least one blackboard myself as a child, so I can warn you not to spend a lot of money on the first slate. As your child matures and learns the difference between paper and the blackboard, you can substitute a larger and better board. They are perfect as wall hangings if placed at a height where they can be easily reached. Portable types are also available.

Blackboards are available from BEKA, Galt Toys, Little Tikes, Small World Toys, and TC Timber. $3–$13.

## 17. Bubble Pipes

Bubble pipes and wands are longtime favorites and probably among the more inexpensive items recommended. You can purchase an already-made bubble-making solution or do your own from mild soap and water. Put the liquid in a plastic container and take it (yourself) outside. The child blows through the pipe or waves the wand to create the bubbles. The pipes make bigger bubbles and give the child greater control, but the wand allows for bubble dancing, kid style. Demonstrate. She'll get a kick watching you blow bubbles. So will you.

Bubble pipes are made by Battat, Funrise, Gordy, Small World Toys, and Tootsie Toy (Strombecker). $1–3.

## 18. Household Objects

Select smaller, lightweight, inexpensive pots and pans—no glass or cast iron; stainless steel is not only too heavy, but a bit expensive for play use. Put covers on top or stack them inside each other. They will make a racket, but that's part of the attraction. Encourage both your little boy and little girl to "cook" with their kitchenware.

Try a rolling pin, wooden spoon, nonbreakable measuring cups, with a small "cutting" board and clay, and your child can roll out an extra "crust" while you are preparing dinner. A wooden spoon can be used to stir; the plastic bowls hold it, and a plastic container contains leftovers. You can also obtain a play iron and ironing board.

Plates and cups are available in sets and stimulate more domestic play. With them, the child will create "tea parties" for friends and dolls. Include plastic spoons, forks, and knives for the completion of the play meal at the play table. Let the child use any of your old place mats and napkins or obtain some from Goodwill. Your toddler will be delighted.

You can find household objects made by Fisher-Price, Galt Toys, PlaySkool, Rubbermaid, and Tupperware. $2–$15.

## 19. Jacks-in-the-Box

Nonthreatening surprises delight your toddler, especially when she discovers that when she turns a crank on a box a figure will pop out of the top. You do not want the figure to startle the child unpleasantly, so introduce it slowly and without too much drama. The surprise, laughter, and immediate "Again!" will erupt swiftly.

This toy is a classic and part of all of our memories. Manufacturers include Bullyland, Fisher-Price, and PlaySkool. $6–$10.

## 20. Musical Instruments and Boxes

If a child is exposed early to music of all kinds, he will usually enjoy listening to it and dancing to it throughout his life. From the baby's first experience with a musical windup teddy bear or music box, he is fascinated by musical sounds. As he grows, a music box which he can operate himself rivets his attention and can be useful to distract him when you change his activity, especially around nap time.

Bells, tambourines, or drums encourage your youngster's active participation. He may like to play along to music on a record player, cassette, or radio. There may be some bite-the-bullet times for you amidst dissonance and very random tempos, but you just might discover your offspring shows signs of musical aptitude! (And it's unlikely you can discover this without allowing your child latitude with music-making toys.)

Experiences in music are important to the child, and can teach her rhythmic movement, singing, and, by singing with other children, bonding. Whether you are of the nature that feels free to dance about or hum or sing to yourself as you do tasks, or prefer listening to music for relaxation and enjoyment, your child will discern that this is a natural way of life and be a more ready participant.

Instruments are available from Battat, Casio, Fisher-Price, Hohner, PlaySkool, Rhythm Band, and Woodstock Percussion. $4–$15.

## 21. Peg-Boards

Using a Peg-Board promotes mastery over simple tasks and is a good for focusing and small-muscle exercise. When your child sees the results, she has a sense of completion and accomplishment. Like blocks, pegs are perfect for teaching manual dexterity, hand/eye coordination, and sequencing. Pegs can be small for older children, but they also come in larger sizes and different colors for younger ones. They fit into holes drilled into boards and children can arrange them as they want. You yourself can also create rows and designs of colors with your child. It's a great stress-buster.

As she grows older and understands colors and numbers, she can be encouraged to make a whole row of the same color and other patterns. Easy-grip pegs are made by some manufacturers, but are usually only available in school-supply stores.

Pegs and boards are available from Anatex, BRIO, Galt Toys, and TC Timber. $5–$10.

## 22. Play Figures

Play people, mannequins, and/or animals made from cloth, plastic, or wood are used for imaginary play and stimulate youngsters to create elaborate stories and role-play with the figures. Some figures come in complete sets: villages, hospitals, farms, schools, and so forth. Get large figures if your child is still putting everything in his mouth.

Some play sets come with very small figures and must be avoided for children who are too young and in danger of swallowing them. Ultimately, any toy can be risky if used improperly, so as you introduce toys, pay attention to the label on the package suggesting age range and make yourself aware of potential hazards.

Play figures are made by BRIO, Fanny's Playhouse, Fisher-Price, Galt Toys, Little Tikes, and PlaySkool. $2–$5.

## 23. Puppets

Puppets teach verbal and social skills and provide awareness of body-language messages. Soft and pliable, they are effective in your youngster's imaginative play. Children use puppets throughout the growing years for acting out stories they make up themselves.

Your little one will play with puppets alone or with others. Puppet play is an acceptable way to release upsets or feelings, and these toys offer your child opportunities for communication and exercising imagination. I recommend starting with simple hand puppets that are not too complicated to work.

If Sesame Street characters are your child's favorites, select one or two such as Big Bird or Cookie Monster, Elmo, Oscar, or Kermit, but don't overdo it. Select generic puppets, too, so the child can create whatever character he wants it to be.

Be sure eyes are sewn on the puppet securely, and other small parts cannot come loose. Fashion a puppet yourself to represent people or animals known personally to your offspring.

Puppets are made by Animal Fair, Eden, Fanny's Playhouse, Fisher-Price, Folkmanis, GUND, Manhattan Toy, and Steiff. $3–$10.

## 24. Telephones

Language skills expand daily, as does your child's consciousness. She listens, observes, and practices everything she hears. A toy telephone assists in developing verbal skills, because a toddler imitates others and will imitate telephone use by making sounds, pressing buttons, dialing, and talking.

Your child may walk around the house with the toy phone dragging and will generously offer you her instrument so she can watch you make calls and talk to daddy and friends. When she does this, do make that call and play along. Your daughter will learn a great deal from your level of playfulness. Play with your child by using the phone with her. This activity can result in a child who will enlarge her vocabulary and speak sentences sooner.

Toy telephones are available with bells or without.

Play telephones are made by BRIO, Chicco, Fisher-Price, and PlaySkool. $5–$10.

## 25. Tops

These are a longtime favorite for many children. Some tops just spin, others spin as musical sounds play, and still others move when the plunger is pushed down. Start with a large, well-balanced one that your child will find easy to make turn. This activity helps develop fine-motor coordination.

Tops are made by Battat, BRIO, Fisher-Price, PlaySkool, and Small World Toys. $5–$10.

## 26. Transportation Toys

With such a wide variety to choose from, you should have no trouble finding your toddler some memorable vehicles. Inspect carefully for sturdiness and test your selection before buying it. Companies which make the better toy vehicles take great pains to be certain their products have smooth edges, are easy for young children to operate, and have a solid center of balance.

Children play with vehicles with imagination and child-generated sounds. Your youngster will create activities around her vehicles, become very absorbed in operating them, and act out all sorts of travel scenarios. If these toys are going to be taken outdoors, get hard plastic ones or those with a rustproof finish. The oversized foot-powered vehicles are great for exercise and provide for imaginative play. Be sure the one you select is well-balanced and manageable.

Features are important, so be sure there is a ladder on the fire truck, the doors to the cab open and close, and the garbage truck lifts and dumps. Make sure the cars are large and rugged. Select different kinds for both city and country drama—for example, a farm tractor and a town dump truck—and show your child the difference to spark her own imagination. Some vehicles can be expensive if you want good quality, so investigate thoroughly. Both girls and boys enjoy playing with transport devices, figures, and play sets.

Transportation toys are made by BRIO, Ertl, Galoob, Hasbro, Holgate, Little Tikes, Mattel, Radio Flyer, TC Timber, Today's Kids, and TYCO. $20–$25.


## 27. Wagons

As toddlers move more easily under their own power, they love to push and pull a wagon with a favorite stuffed animal, doll, or other plaything inside. The classic wagon in wood, metal, or plastic is exactly right for this purpose. Be sure to get one that has good balance, secure wheels, and offers enough space to load up.

Don't start out by buying one that is too big, as it will be frustrating for the child. Consider not only its size but its weight, balance, and easy maneuverability.

Excellent wagons are made by Little Tikes, Radio Flyer, and Today's Kids. $20–$50.

## 28. Wooden Beads

Beads are available in different colors and shapes. When playing with them, the child is learning color, shapes, and gaining hand/ eye coordination. Large wooden beads provide manual activity for the older toddler as she creates wampum, lamp-shade covers, necklaces, and the like. Many preschoolers want to string beads as soon as they can thread the holes. If your child does not seem interested, put the beads away for several months.

Stay with your little one when you first show him the new beads and how they can work. Be sure to make a large knot at the end of the string so beads cannot fall off the end. Let him discover how to make the rest. He may add five or ten beads and then lose interest for a time, but he will come back to the challenge if you do not push the activity. If you make a necklace for a doll he will get the idea and may make one for each of his stuffed animals.

Beads are made by Galt Toys, PlaySkool, and TC Timber. $5–$8.

SUGGESTED ADDITIONAL PRODUCTS THAT BUILD SKILLS:

- Dapper Dan and Dressy Bessy Dolls (for dressing skills)
- Giant Links (dexterity)
- Play sets (communication)
- Rocking horse (coordination)
- See 'N' Say (educational fun)
- Shoe lacing (dexterity)
- Snap-lock beads (dexterity)
- Wood pieces (creativity)

## ▶ DEVELOPMENTAL MILESTONES OF TODDLERS

## Physical

- Sturdy on feet.
- Bends at waist to pick up objects.
- Can travel up and down stairs without alternating feet.
- Can rotate forearm, so can turn doorknobs.
- Pinches, pushes, kicks, bites.
- Usually dry at night.
- Can take off shoes, stockings, pants.
- Dawdles because she is not well coordinated.

## Emotional/Social

- Negativistic; exercises powers.
- Fear of bed-wetting, animals, being deserted.
- Feelings of helplessness.
- Temper tantrums; attempts to control.
- Fussy eater.
- Ritualistic and self-centered.
- Cannot share ("It's mine"); possessive.
- Shows pity, sympathy, modesty.
- Can feel shame and evidence guilt.
- Difficulty with choices.
- Hesitant with strangers.
- Experiments with independence.
- Spends a good bit of time absorbed in gazing.
- Is warmly responsive, loving, and affectionate.
- Dependent on mother or other adult.
- Sometimes lacking in self-confidence.
- Shows signs of possessiveness and aggressive behavior.

## Mental

- Vocabulary increases to about three hundred words.
- Begins sentences and three-word phrases.
- Skilled imitation and mimicry.
- Responds to humor or distraction.
- Resents punishments, especially when unclear.
- Creates singsong phrases of two to three words.
- Knows own name.
- Questions "What's this?" "What's that?"
- Knows names: things, persons, actions, situations.
- Uses some adverbs, adjectives, and prepositions.
- Asks for table items using name of article.
- Tells needs, but does not converse.
- Responds to suggestions better than commands.
- Can accept imaginary pleasures.
- Concentrates interest in small areas.
- Attention is in present; future is a dim concept.

## PLAY POINTS

- Use sponges, plastic cups, and washcloths, plus a few small floating toys, in the bathtub for variety.
- Use a board on a slant to give the child an incline to use with cars and trucks.
- Create time for music, active movement, and outdoor play every day.
- Allow the child a chance to "cook" or "bake" when you do (and when he is old enough he'll be ready to learn the real thing).
- Give small numbers/amounts of utensils and ingredients: a plastic bowl, a palmful of clay, a wooden spoon.
- Be sure to talk, sing, play with, and read to your growing child.

- Attention span is about two to three minutes.
- Responds to familiar adults.
- Holds hands while walking.
- "Helps" around the house.

## At Play

- Enjoys books, music, blocks.
- Can kick a ball.
- Can build a tower of six to seven blocks.
- Solitary to parallel play.
- Intrigued by water.
- Likes humor games, such as peekaboo and chasing.
- Can copy a circle.
- Carries on "conversation" with doll or stuffed toy.
- Likes to touch and look at books.
- Can identify many pictures by name.
- Enjoys repetition, nonsense rhymes.
- Sees and reaches out at same time.
- Locates pictures in picture book.
- Fits nested blocks together.
- Takes things apart and fits them together again.
- Can run, pull, push, drag, squat, clap in rhythm.
- Can kick a ball and catch with arms.
- Needs to be near adult in play-group situations.
- Asks adult for something wanted from another child.
- Does not yet cooperate well.
- Unlikely to share; may engage in tugs-of-war.
- Collects and hangs on to toys.
- Enjoys dramatic play; imagination can be vivid.
- Doesn't often distinguish between play and reality.

## ▶ MENTAL MILESTONES AT TWO AND ONE-HALF YEARS

### Physical

- Jumps on both feet.
- Tiptoes.
- Holds pencil more correctly; imitates strokes.
- Bowel and bladder control accomplished.

### Emotional/Social

- Goes to extremes in all things.
- Realizes life has alternatives.
- Resists being forced.
- Does not share willingly.
- Unpredictable.
- Dawdles when can't make a choice.

### Mental

- Vocabulary increased to about one thousand words.

### At Play

- Dramatic and parallel play.
- Tower of eight blocks and simple bridges.

# FOUR

# Preschooler

## BETWEEN THREE AND FIVE YEARS OLD

When Barbara and Tom talked with me about their four-year-old, they were concerned about the child's shyness with other children. Barbara feared that her daughter, Tara, would not socially adjust well in the nursery school she was to be enrolled in shortly. I suggested taking time to play with puppets as one way of encouraging the child to expand her own voice and to find comfort in communicating.

In addition, I suggested that Barbara and Tom spend time reading to their little girl so she would become more familiar with language. I also encouraged the family to invite a neighbor child or two over for Tara to play with as this would accustom her to easy play with other children.

Soon Tara began to open up in her conversations with her new friend and through puppet play. Barbara and Tom saw to it that Tara discovered the fun of interactive play with another child while they were there to lend familiarity. The adjustment to nursery school became easier as a result of the support she received beforehand. Her parents also learned more about child development as their child's Play Tutors. With that understanding, they began to relax in dealing with the various stages through which their daughter, Tara, was moving.

## More Sophisticated Interests

Preschoolers love creative playthings: finger paints, chalkboards, and drawing equipment. They enjoy playing with dolls and puppets and like to examine interesting objects. This is a time when children enjoy constructing things and improve their ability to use the materials with which they play. The ability to draw the things your child sees—daddy, mommy, brother, house, cat—becomes more focused and she improves her perceptions, as well as the rendering of them.

The preschooler becomes more involved in complicated dramatic and fantasy play and he enjoys creating characters, drawing from his experiences with family and friends. Dress-up mannequins or dolls with zippers, laces to tie, and snaps to fasten help your young one to expand his self-help skills.

The child of four and five years is facile with ride-ons, wagons, and tricycles as she gains in gross motor skills. She likes the ones that look like horses, cars, motorcycles, trains, or spacecraft. She will delight in pulling wagons with things inside of them. However, watch her carefully; she may tend to wander off easily.

The preschooler's imagination is broadening, so puppets, dolls, mannequins, and telephones take on new and complex meaning. He loves to dress up and have play clothes, fabrics, and hats to put on. He finds that acting out "store," "house," and "going on a trip" with other children is a favored pasttime and this is when the preschooler is drawn to other children for group play. Nursery schools, child-care centers, Head Start centers, and play groups at home are of great value. The child at this age is comfortable with friends, and though they may fight or have disagreements, these are of brief duration. Now she begins to comprehend the give-and-take of sharing activities and toys, taking turns, and adapting to new friends. She acts in a more socially acceptable manner with others.

Boys and girls are now growing at about the same rate. The expansion of the long muscles is a noticeable part of their overall physical development.

Preschoolers use more outdoor equipment than ever before: swings, ride-ons, and climbing structures. During this period the child can run, jump, climb, and bounce with skill and precision. He has more strength, durability, adeptness, coordination, and the ability to repeat movements.

## Concentration Improvements

Attention span has grown and he can concentrate on tasks for a longer period of time. Some of the quiet activities he prefers are games, puzzles, simple crafts like braiding belts, easy sewing or a craft kit, and building with construction toys.

Three- and four-year-old children understand what is being said by others, but will vary in their own ability to talk and express ideas. They love to listen to read-aloud stories and have favorites which they'll ask for time and time again, so be prepared. Tape their favorite stories for repeat appeal when you cannot read in person. The preschooler delights in make-believe games: being the hero of his own drama, playing the parts of mom, dad, baby, and other significant persons in his life.

By now your youngster can learn the sounds of the alphabet and absorb simple abstractions (i.e., the letter *C* starts the word *cat*, but also does much more). Having colorful magnetic letters on the refrigerator door encourages her to recognize and play with letters and to make up easy words (dog, I, you, love, mom, dad). This leads to earlier and better reading skills for most kids.

In fact, three basic rules apply:

1. *Read aloud* to him daily if possible.
2. *Keep reading materials in plain sight* around the house in quantity—books, magazines, newspapers.
3. *Don't hide your own reading* under a bushel of tasks, talk, and TV.

There is plenty of evidence that helping a child establish a strong reading habit can raise her IQ—a measurement of *ability* to learn, not a measurement of knowledge achieved—by ten to fifteen points. Reading aloud and playing with a toy that fits the book can be a great way to encourage your child's reading interest and skill.

The concepts of time, space, volume, and quantity take longer for most children to acquire. Don't push these abstractions before your child is ready to grasp them. Allow him the experiences of time passing, of space to travel, of bunches of stuff that can be held before dropping, and of how many raisins mommy will allow—these experiences do the teaching (with no more than casual explanations from you); let your child set his own pace.

## Emotional Ricochets and Early Learning

Expressions of anger and frustration are natural during play. Puppets, dolls, and dollhouses make these feelings safer, less anxious, and more comfortable for the child. A younger child, infant or toddler, may discharge anger through temper tantrums. As he begins to reason, he'll become more verbal than physical.

If, however, her anger is expressed in unacceptable ways—throwing a toy and breaking it or something else—your reaction is vital. Rather than showing anger yourself, show sympathy for the breaking of the toy and do discard it. Do not replace it. Help your child see an inevitable consequence: Toy is *gone!*

It is possible, now, to help him focus the empathy skills that, as Play Tutor, you've helped him acquire. It is time for your child to comprehend another's hurt, frustration, resentment, or anger. If he wounds another, either accidentally or deliberately, he must be shown this is not acceptable, and given to understand that there are limits to his behavior and what those limits are. These limits must be consistent regardless of whether at home or preschool, on the playground, or visiting. Observe him and listen to him. Learn about the issues with which he is trying to cope. Don't make snap judgments. In the cases of incidents of misbehavior reported to you by others, before taking action find out exactly what happened, not just from your child's perspective, but from the viewpoint of the person complaining. In these instances, reality is typically somewhere in between the two accounts. Be wise, don't overcondemn your youngster, but also do not be overprotective. Balance is not always easy to achieve in parenting, but it is an important goal. In the long run your child will benefit if you are fair.

For example, if you see that your child is in the wrong in an altercation with another child, help her to see this in a gentle, nonrejecting way. Some of the worst damage loving parents can do to their child is giving misplaced "loyalty" by defending what is wrong as if it were right. Help her learn now and throughout her growing years (and yes, even when she's an adult—we never stop being parents, you know) that being wrong isn't what's terrible and is even forgivable. The worst thing about being wrong is not admitting it and not making it right if possible.

Your coaching job becomes critical during such episodes. You must, at times, contain your own angry feelings because you are mentor and example for your young one. It is a chilling experience to see your beloved child mimic your own less admirable behavior.

This is also a period when sibling rivalry might escalate. Jane and Paul noticed that their children, ages two and four, liked many of the same activities, but were also having many conflicts. The differences in the styles and abilities of the little girls frustrated the younger child, who, typically, tried to copy her sibling.

I worked with Jane and Paul to help them present their two

children with less competitive activities. We focused on what both children could do together without being compared to each other.

For example, instead of both kids attempting the same task, each should perform what she can do well as a part of a greater, joint endeavor. Jane cut varying lengths of wool for two rag dolls she was making for each child. Jenny, age four, sorted the strands into piles of the same length. Beth, two and a half, put each pile into a different receptacle mom had prepared: six empty baskets. The tasks were geared to each child's ability; they did not conflict, yet were part of a single joint project.

Another solution to sibling rivalry is providing each child duplicates of a few favorite toys. This way parents can ease competition. Children can have positive play in close proximity if you do some preparation beforehand.

## Playing with Peers

A play group gives your child a chance to role-play with other children whom he knows and trusts. Preschoolers learn more in these groups than they can alone or with just one or two playmates.

Imaginary companions are common at this age, especially with the firstborn or only child. Fantasy playmates emerge as a natural part of inventiveness and they will be around for a while. Do not be alarmed, since mythical playmates are part of normal emotional growth.

Your child will find his own pace as he plays, but he needs you and teacher to make sure he does not get overstimulated. The three-year-old will ask many, many questions so be patient with his curiosity. He wants to know everything about this world that is so rapidly unfolding.

She feels good about herself and she will express her growing confidence in, perhaps, not acceptable ways. Try not to say "no" to her in an irritated tone, but do be firm—mean it! Don't ask—tell! Limit "nos" to important things, rather than for inconvenient, but not harmful, behaviors. Your child needs positive reinforcement while building self-confidence by taking risks and trying things in new situations that will provide new and enriched experiences. Encourage her to try things that you know she can handle.

Periods during the ages of three to five are, for many children, a magical time and a time their parents will look back upon with fondness. Preschoolers are usually cooperative, and do not challenge instructions. They will generally go along, be easy to talk to, and are customarily not hard to get along with. If your child seems to be an exception to this, though, don't worry. Mild willfulness may indicate a precocious mind.

The picture may change quickly, as early as within six months. The child finds it important to establish his identity and will say "no" a lot, so it may become harder to get cooperation. It is a natural shift in the developing personality, so don't be worried or wonder, "Where did my nice little boy go?"

These personality changes continue throughout childhood. They are simply what happens developmentally and naturally within each child. Your understanding of what is normal, such as an outwardly secure child suddenly becoming insecure and uncertain, a happy child becoming moody, or an easy child becoming stubborn, are all part of the changing, shifting patterns of growth. These changes can be confusing and frustrating to you at times, but if you relax and do not get upset, most of these temporary mood shifts will change by themselves.

Sometimes these changes, however, can be indications of potential problems. For example, if a particular behavior persists over a longer period, and your child seems more frequently upset, pay attention to what might be specifically causing this and discuss it with your pediatrician.

For the most part, however, inconsistency is a natural part of the growing-up adventure. Children outgrow temporary changes. Do not take it personally, and allow your child to express her feelings in a reasonable way. Talk with her or distract her if she's being unreasonable, and in cases of more profound antisocial behavior, devise reasonable consequences that she will understand.

Never, *never*, confuse "reasonable consequences" with what is really a venting of your own anger. He will sense this and no matter how correct you are in the decision to stem his action you cannot be effective if he can detect any *un*reasonableness in yours. And do not make the mistake of underestimating your preschooler. His awareness is probably far more sophisticated than his language skills.

Understand that the preschool child's emotions and behaviors can shift rapidly from happy to sad, from quiet to active. Do not argue with your child; see if both of you can be winners. Provide alternatives and positive support. It cannot be emphasized strongly enough that good behavior be rewarded as much as, if not more than, bad behavior receives consequences. A new small toy can sometimes be an appreciative reinforcement for a child's efforts when she is especially helpful and cooperative or performs other good behavior worth noting. A child needs to believe she has "won" on occasion; it is part of her building inner strength, power, and self-esteem.

I had an uncle who did not subscribe to the concept of compensating good behavior. He was of the "virtue is its own reward" school, and as out of touch with modern approaches as this seems, even today I can detect a logical point behind this. There has to be a fine line drawn between approval and bribery. Giving a toy for every gold star (or, when he is older, paying him for each "A" or "B") comes suspiciously close to instilling an undesirable acquisitiveness.

It is never too early to help your child *feel* the exhilaration that comes with pride of achievement, which can't be matched by his feelings of acquiring any material thing. The preschool age is a time when your child wants and needs your approval, and *showing* that approval with smiles and hugs and a display of your pride in him is more often the best reward you can give your child.

The preschooler *wants* to get along and to comprehend how others feel. This is a milestone for cooperative play and, for the most part, she will get along with other children if she is not subjected to being too frequently "the new kid on the block." Changes of schools or major moves to a new town will mean a period of her trying to assimilate into already established peer structures. In cases where such moves are unavoidable, extra awareness and support on your part is necessary.

When children play together, they imitate each other and learn from each other's behavior, interests, and responses. They copy each other's silliness and delight in taking turns at the imitative-type games they create.

By understanding the variety of play your child likes at this age, you can better plan the types of toys to have available at home. Observe her play at her play group and at nursery school. She is physically very active: climbing, playing with large blocks, tricycles, and wagons. She likes to create things with finger paints, soap bubbles, clay, collages, yarn pictures, and cutouts. And although many of these playthings were introduced when she was younger, she is now engaged in far more complex activities with them.

## Activities for Parent and Child

Playing games with your young one who is three, four, or five years old creates a happy, bonding time that will not again be as easy. Games will not only bring you both pleasure but will broaden his horizons of knowledge—and yours. Here are some suggestions:

- Close your eyes and ask him to tell you what is in the room. Add the topics of colors or shapes later in the game.
- Teach her songs and sing together.
- Tell each other stories that you each make up; play "Chapters"—one starts a "chapter" (story segment), the other com-

## TOY SUGGESTIONS FOR PRESCHOOLERS THREE TO FOUR YEARS OLD

1. Art supplies                      (C)
2. Balls and beanbags                (A)
3. Beads                             (E)
4. Blocks                            (A)
5. Books                             (E)
6. Construction toys                 (A)
7. Dolls and action figures          (E)
8. Housekeeping toys                 (E)
9. Music and instruments             (C)
10. Play people and play sets        (E)
11. Puzzles                          (E)
12. Sandbox and outdoor toys         (A)
13. Stuffed animals                  (C)
14. Transportation toys              (E)
15. Tricycles                        (A)

pletes it and starts a new chapter, which the first completes. Continue until someone says "and they lived happily ever after."

- Have "jokefests": imagine silly things and laugh about them together.
- Begin a picture and let your child finish it, and vice versa.
- Create things together from clay or construction toys.

Excellent preschool toys are available. The following are suggestions. The balance between active, creative, and educational products as discussed on pages 15 and 16 is always important.

## 1. Art Supplies

Art expression is self-expression. Media appropriate for preschoolers are: paint, clay, paper (for collages and simple origami), finger paint, glue, pictures, and yarn. She will need brushes and scissors and miscellaneous materials with which to work. Keep these supplies in a place where she can locate them easily. Organize them in boxes so they are readily available, but always see that your child uses them under supervision. There's no telling what can happen if you leave children alone with paints. However, you don't have to stop everything you are doing to supervise. Let your child play nearby with clay or water paints while you are cooking or reading or doing other not too demanding tasks. Be flexible, however, about interruptions and frequent requests for help, and when she must share her creations. Ask your child periodically during these times to tell you about what she is doing, if she has not already done so.

Create an area where you can display his artwork. He will feel pride in what he has done and will want to do more, and you just may be encouraging a burgeoning Picasso. Give him the time he might need to finish his project, but be sensitive to signs of tiring and invite him to complete it later.

You can obtain art supplies in any five-and-dime, teaching-supply, art, or office-supply store, and in most toy stores. You don't have to spend a lot of money to get a good variety of supplies.

Art sets contain nontoxic paints, crayons, or colored pencils, and will often suggest art activities. Brown butcher paper, newsprint, nonstick white shelf paper, and brown wrapping-paper rolls are excellent for paint activities; a roll of such paper goes a long way.

Consider also templates and shapes, like Colorform shapes, or rubber stamps to print and make patterns.

Locate a good supply of clay, Play-Doh, or plasticine, or make your own:

## DR. TOY'S RECIPE FOR EASY, PLAY CLAY

2 cups flour
$2/3$ cup salt
$1/2$ cup water
a few drops of vegetable oil
a few drops of vegetable coloring or nontoxic, washable paint

Stir flour, salt, water, and vegetable oil and separate into smaller batches for different colors. Mix in safe vegetable coloring or nontoxic, washable paint to each of the batches and then knead until smooth. Store in airtight container at room temperature.

OTHER ART SUPPLIES:

- Blackboard and various colors of chalk.
- Bulletin board (for displaying child's art).
- Easel: There are floor tripods, floor T-braced easels, and table models available. Be sure the one you choose is well-balanced, weighted adequately, and not easily tipped over.
- Etch-A-Sketch, Colorforms, Rolocolor coloring desk, and a Magna Doodle.
- Sponges, brushes, DoodleTops, and other materials to apply paints (including fingers).

Art supplies for children are made by ALEX, All Night Media, Avalon, Binney & Smith, Colorforms, Dixon Ticonderoga, DoodleTop, Fisher-Price, Fiskars, Hero Arts, Kenner, and Reeves International. $1–$15.

## 2. Balls and Beanbags

The child at this age likes throwing balls, beanbags, and Koosh balls. Big beach balls, large sponge balls, and Nerf balls are favorites. They are relatively inexpensive, last a long time, and provide entertainment and exercise.

Balls are great for large- and small-muscle development. They promote facility and precision of movement, and provide practice for coordination. Positive social play advances: It takes at least two to play ball!

A good indoor game for a rainy day is throwing a beanbag into a target (use a clean, empty plastic trash can or cardboard container) and gradually moving the target longer distances away. Plan to supervise or participate in this and choose an area devoid of breakables.

You can buy beanbags or make your own. Be sure they are well secured, whether purchased or made by yourself, or you will have beans flying everywhere.

Look for balls from Battat, Come Play Products, Just Toys, Oddzon, Small World Toys, and TC Timber. $1–$6.

## 3. Beads

Large wooden beads for making necklaces or ropes are now easier for children to manipulate. Beads teach colors, shapes, coordination, and fine-motor ability, and help your child learn to count. Playing with beads is a quiet indoor activity and good for a rainy day. Creating beadwork is a quiet-time activity good to balance the rough-and-tumble play in which preschoolers often engage.

Be sure to tie the end of the string with a large knot so the beads do not slip off. You will notice in activities like bead-stringing that your child improves his ability to manipulate and coordinate finger movements.

You can obtain beads from ALEX, Pastime, and PlaySkool, or in bulk from craft and hobby specialty stores. $5–$8.

## 4. Blocks

Blocks are one of the best long-term smart-play investments you can make. These simple products continue to give your child much to play with and to stretch her imagination. They come in all sizes and materials from small, plain wooden ones in primary colors, through those with letters and pictures, to large foam and plastic forms, either plain or colored, or in the shape of real bricks.

Preschoolers choose blocks to create marvelous constructions: playhouses for dolls, garages for cars, and imaginary buildings that may not be explainable, but are beautifully fabricated. Have a place set up for your youngster to store his blocks or everyone will trip over them, and that's not fun.

**PLAY POINT:** Ask your child to tell you about his creations, but do not interfere or make strong suggestions. He will build and destroy at his whim and this gives him the feeling that he is in control, has power. Such impulses are survival tools; you must prepare to balance between sanctioning them and teaching him how to use impulses appropriately.

Blocks offer all the elements of smart play—creative, active, and educational—in one product. They are one of many excellent open-ended child-centered toys.

You can obtain blocks from Community Playthings, Fisher-Price, Holgate, Little Tikes, Mattel, PlaySkool, TC Timber, Uncle Goose, and WJ Fantasy. $7–$25.

## 5. Books

Books are your child's best friends. Through books, as opposed to television, her creative mind will be stimulated continuously: Her imagination is ignited by reading about places she's never been, things she's never seen, people she's never known. Your young one will absorb ideas and concepts, puzzle out and analyze problems, create original visualizations, and become a better all-round learner through reading.

From books the child gains skills he will use the rest of his life. He will develop and express preferences about a multitude of things from liking koala bears to disliking snakes, from being intrigued by astronomy to being bored by crop rotation.

Your little girl learns a great deal besides the "what ifs" of a story from hearing you read aloud. She will become familiar with the cadence of words, the flow of sentences, and the sharpness of dialogue. The descriptions of settings she has never encountered will broaden her imagination and ability to "envision" new things. Finally, as she matures she will become eager to read for herself, if for no other reason than that mom or dad simply doesn't have time enough to *read* enough to satisfy her insatiable curiosity about "What happens next?"!

Reading aloud is an ideal activity to share together. As a quiet, nonstimulating, but attention-holding device it's a perfect way to quiet an active child before nap or bedtime. Patterns of activity are appealing to a child this age, and putting things away, bathing, brushing teeth and hair, listening to music, and then reading together with mommy or daddy before bedtime is a ritual that makes good habits, good hygiene, a good night, and good dreams.

Take your preschooler to the library and to bookstores. Teach him how to browse (and teach him about "quiet time"—no loud talk, just whispers, in these special places). Don't stay too long, and give him your total attention; save the selection of your own books for a time he isn't with you. He'll get a negative impression of book "houses" if the librarian has to ride herd on him for disturbing other patrons. And don't forget to look up local story-time events; attend them at the bookstore, the toy shop, or the library.

Some excellent books are *Cat in the Hat, The Complete Adventures of Winnie-the-Pooh, A Bear Called Paddington, Snoopy, The Adventures of Raggedy Ann and Andy,* and the *Thomas the Tank Engine* stories. Buy a Pooh bear, a stuffed Snoopy, Thomas, or another toy that matches the book and make it a part of read-aloud time.

The preschooler can now also handle more complicated and

longer read-aloud stories like *Charlotte's Web*, *The Wizard of Oz*, *The Little Engine That Could*, and *The Cat in the Hat* and likes to hear them repeated and read the same way each time. She likes funny stories that make her laugh, stories that reflect the experiences she's having, and stories of adventures.

The picaresque story engages the four- and five-year-old and older child. These are tales of charming rogues and their episodic adventures with, usually on a second level, satirically realistic detail about everyday life. These are the books that entertain adults on one level while riveting the child's attention at a simpler

**PLAY POINT:**
Research indicates that children whose parents take the time to read to them early have fewer problems learning to read later on and do better overall in school achievement.

one. Examples are *Gulliver's Travels*, *Don Quixote*, *The Adventures of Tom Sawyer*, *The Princess Bride*, and *Zorro*, which can be obtained in adaptation (simpler prose) for the preschooler, but can be read aloud to your child in the original within a surprisingly few years (when he is eight or nine). Bear in mind that children—and adults—comprehend large words that are well in advance of their speaking vocabularies; and all vocabulary is painlessly augmented when the unfamiliar words are in the context of an interesting story.

Examine any book before purchase for illustrations, text, messages—overt or hidden—and decide if it is a book your child will comprehend and take pleasure from, and one that *you* will enjoy reading to her.

For the young preschooler, try to get washable, sturdy books. If you receive a gift of a book you do not feel is right for your child, exchange it for one that is more appropriate or donate it to the library. Be sure to have a place in the child's room or play area where he can put away his books and store and retrieve them easily. Be sure to take your child to the public library to obtain a card in his or her name and attend story hours in the children's section. The American Library Association has many helpful publications available on the importance of reading. The children's librarian can refer you to more publications and other information about reading.

Books for children can be obtained from Bobbs-Merrill; Dawn Publishing; Delacourte; Dorling Kindersley; Doubleday; EDC; Firefly Books; Follet; Golden Books; Grosset & Dunlap; Harcourt Brace; HarperCollins; Henry Holt; Houghton Mifflin; Klutz; Knopf; Little, Brown; McGraw-Hill; Mudpuppy; Penguin; Planet Dexter; Rand McNally; Random House; Scholastic; Sierra Club Books; Silver Burdett; Spizzirri Publishing; John Wiley; WJ Fantasy; and Workman. $2–$10.

## 6. Construction Toys

Like blocks, construction toys allow children maximum imaginative activity and the chance to create. They come in plastic or wood and with many differently shaped components. Try not to interfere or give directions unless your youngster has a question or asks for help.

Occasionally join in play. Do a different construction while your child is busy making one. Your company will be welcomed and he'll notice what you are doing and how, and often be inspired to new creations from your quiet, parallel play with him. Make positive comments about his work but explain your own only if he queries you.

Construction activities provide problem-solving and coordination skills. Your preschooler will create, take apart, and start all over again. Let him have plenty of time to devise original structures; who knows, he may someday become a future Frank Lloyd Wright, a designer, a civil engineer, or an architect.

Your daughter benefits equally from these experiences. She may have the same aspirations to be an architect or engineer. One never knows what may prompt a child's decisions and shape the rest of her life. These are the times that allow her to expand mental, physical, and creative horizons.

For this age start with selections from BRIO, Duplo by Lego, and PlaySkool. $5–$25.

## 7. Dolls and Action Figures

One of the most phenomenal segments of the entire toy industry is the number and variety of excellent dolls being manufactured. They range from soft fabric dolls, small figures, and shapely designer dolls to robust baby dolls, costumed creations, and action mannequins. The play value of dolls is endless and the collecting possibilities are beyond the imagination.

Doll collectors' groups are found throughout the U.S. and Europe; collecting is an active hobby for many. You may want to select collector dolls as part of your child's toy treasures and start building as an early investment for her.

Dolls are not exclusive to little girls. Boys are drawn to action figures. The classic dolls for boys are toy soldiers and are equally collectible, especially historical sets that represent great battles; these need not teach warlike attitudes if you are involved with intro-

**PLAY POINT:** Dad might create a bed for the baby doll, Mom crochet or sew a doll blanket, and you might consider obtaining a child- and doll-size chair and table for your child and his or her dolly to play together. Playing mommy or daddy and putting the baby to sleep, eating with, and talking to the doll are activities common to almost every youngster of this age.

ducing them and engage in your child's early play with them. You set the tone. Toy soldiers can teach forethought, strategy, relationships—and may be a springboard for expressing ideals important to you for your child.

At this age, for practical everyday use a basic doll is one of the best playthings, especially for the younger child. An inexpensive baby doll with a soft touch, simple features, easy to dress, undress, and bathe will delight your child. A soft Superman, Batman, or other hero will also please. Rag dolls like Raggedy Ann and Andy are appropriate. Those special, designer dolls are best saved for later on when your child is more mature. Dolls that provide dressing skills are also great. They have snaps, zippers, Velcro closures, and lacing.

Making dolls for your child is a special pleasure for you both when you involve him with its design and construction. A number of books are available at the library or at a sewing or craft store with easy directions on how to make them. Later on dad may want to build a dollhouse—no mean feat!—or you may decide to purchase one with accessories and artifacts.

Basic housekeeping skills derive from caring for the doll, as does important awareness of family roles. Boys and girls both need the experiences of doll play, which helps them act out their feelings and solidify their sense of identity. You will find your child talking to the doll and making "dolly" very real. And for your child, it *is* very real.

Excellent dolls are available from companies such as Corolle, Eden, Effanbee, Fisher-Price, Goldberger/Eugene, and PlaySkool. $5–$30.

## 8. Housekeeping Toys

At the preschool age, a natural part of playing is acting out familiar roles. This happens at home with friends, at nursery school, or at the child-care center. Acting out different people, situations, and places is the way young children develop language and gain skills in social relationships. You can help your child take even more pleasure from this time by providing simple props: broom, dustpan, a few pots and pans, dishes, play stove, tables and chairs, eating utensils, plastic bowls and cups, play clothes, and play tool sets.

Hats of various kinds help children create changes in the characters they act out.

Your youngster needs a place to store these objects. If he has one place that is exclusive, it will help keep playthings from being underfoot. Don't let the amount of household play equipment get out of hand. Be selective. Children can have fun with a small number of objects. The rest of the equation is their imagination.

When cooking, let your child participate by giving him small amounts of real food to mix, shape, or roll. Children enjoy proximity to you, talking and imitating the activities you are doing. Introduce this early, whether to a boy or girl. If not a *cordon bleu* chef as an adult, your offspring will at least be able to prepare and enjoy her own meals.

When it comes to preparation of items like pancakes or French toast, let your small *sous-chef* learn to mix the eggs, milk, and batter. Later on, he will enjoy eating the food even more because he helped make it.

Household items can be obtained from Galt Toys, International Playthings, Rubbermaid, and Tupperware. $2–$15.

## 9. Music and Instruments

This is definitely the time to expose your child to a variety of musical experiences if you have not already done so. Ideally, you have provided her with music since she was a baby and toddler. By now she should be hearing a variety of music; whatever your favorite music may be, share it with her. Also include classics (or good pop if classics are *your* preference) and folk music, along with children's songs. Music is an art form. Children should hear and experience the gamut for overall, well-rounded growth.

Music is good for children physically, too. They like to hear it, move to it, dance, sing, and clap to it, and play music themselves. Learning music helps your child in many ways. You may find out the type of instrument your child would like to master by exposing him to different instruments and watching his reactions.

Tapes and CDs for children are produced with a whole range of musical offerings. If possible, provide him his own cassette or CD player; let him start his personal cassette and CD collection.

Many inexpensive and sturdy instruments are made expressly for children, and be sure to expose her to an assortment. Let your child help you choose the things she want to hear; later on, as she gains more experience with music, her own tastes will develop. If you dislike hard rock or rap, this is your best chance to expose her to alternatives so that she can appreciate many styles while forming her own preferences. If you wait until her teens, she'll have built-in prejudices from influential peers and may not be approachable on the subject of alternatives.

Teach your child not to touch other people's musical instruments without asking first. It is natural for him to want to touch pianos and pluck guitars (any musical instrument will fascinate). Guide him now to an instrument he can handle and enjoy—and one which he can understand and take care of. Learning music will bring enjoyment throughout your child's life.

A good beginning keyboard is made for children by several companies. Percussion instruments (drums and cymbals) and recorders are also good choices for this age. Instruments and music can be obtained from Battat, Bontempi, Fisher-Price, Hal Leonard, Hohner, Music for Little People, PlaySkool, Proll, Rhythm Band, Rock 'N Learn, Rounder Kids, Twin Sisters Productions, and Woodstock Percussion. $4–$25.

## 10. Play People and Play Sets

Miniature play people in sets offer creative times and intriguing new knowledge. These figures come in a wide range of choices, including western, medieval, and everyday scenes in a community, both modern and historical.

Locate figure sets that include both boys and girls, men and women, and animals. You child can begin collecting these items if you two are so inclined. This is probably too young an age for her to start any serious collections, but the pieces can be enjoyed and treasured.

The commercial play sets are very well done, but you can also make your own. Cardboard for both scenes and simple figures is an excellent medium because it is versatile. Plan your project well before purchasing supplies and be sure the paint you obtain is nontoxic.

By adding small cars, trains, and other playthings (like blocks or construction forms) to a set you have bought or made, you can create a complete village. Your preschooler will be absorbed for hours playing alone or with friends, devising action and movement around these farms and minivillages.

Play sets are available from Battat, BRIO, Fisher-Price, Galoob, Holgate, Little Tikes, PlaySkool, Small World Toys, TC Timber, and Today's Kids. $2–$10.

## 11. Puzzles

As the child matures, he can use jigsaw puzzles with more pieces and complexity. Puzzles are great entertainment on rainy days and for quiet time. If the child is convalescing from illness, use puzzles for an engrossing activity; they are a good substitute for TV. Puzzles teach finger coordination, dexterity, spatial relationships, and logical thinking.

Choose puzzles that children of this age can complete realistically. If the puzzle is too complex, your youngster will be frustrated and not only give it up but assume an unfortunate "I don't like puzzles" perspective. The number of pieces increases proportionally to age and ability. Give your child a tray or table surface which need not be cleared each day on which to lay out the puzzle, and sufficient time to work until she shows signs of tiring of the activity. Make your child aware that it is not vital to complete a jigsaw puzzle at one sitting; that it is a "come back to it" toy.

At times she also may ask for your help, and you should sit down with her and play along for a while. Puzzles are a good mutual activity with each person generally working on a different area of the puzzle, but stopping once in a while to help the other with a segment. For the most part, let your child figure out how to solve the puzzles for herself.

Again, you must be the judge of what is possible and what's not yet within your child's grasp and the best way to do this is to take time to work along with him.

Puzzles are a good item to reassemble after a first completion, as the mood and inclination strikes your child. It will go faster the second time it's worked. For puzzles that were especially challenging to complete and/or those that make up into particularly attractive pictures the assembled puzzle can be permanently adhered together and mounted on poster board for a wall decoration in your child's room. Instructions and supplies for this are available in hobby and crafts shops. Of course these are great items that can be donated to children's programs.

You can find puzzles made by Briarpatch, BRIO, DaMert, Fisher-Price, Frank Schaffer, FX Schmid, Galt Toys, Great American Puzzle Factory, Lauri, Learning Curve, Milton Bradley, PlaySkool, TC Timber, Tootsietoy, and Wrebbit. $3–$10.

## 12. Sandbox and Outdoor Toys

Children need to play in dirt, sand, and water and require at least a bucket and a shovel for this activity. The rest is optional. All summer long, wading pools, rubber balls, hoses, and large plastic containers are simple, accessible, and constantly used playthings for the backyard.

If you wish, you can obtain a number of items and keep them just for outdoor play: watering cans, funnels, egg beaters, and plastic pitchers. Be sure to select items that cannot be broken easily or splintered. Be sure the sand, water, and outdoor areas are kept clean from debris and clear of anything breakable.

Playground equipment at home should be plain and sturdy. A swing, slide, and ladder lead to hours of playtime. Be sure the ground at the base of the equipment is safe, semisoft, and resilient for children's occasional falls. It should be able to cushion a fall safely. Check for buried rocks; hard-packed dirt is equally undesirable. Talk to your local nursery about hardy grass to plant around those areas.

Outdoor toys are available from Air Pogo, Fisher-Price, Hedstrom, Little Tikes, Step 2, and Today's Kids. $35–$150.

## 13. Stuffed Animals

The preschooler is not too old for stuffed animals (and, as has been stated, your child may never be too old for them). This might be time to add to or replace her collection because, long-lasting, cuddly, and emotionally satisfying, the stuffed animal is a most wonderful toy. Like "dolly," "teddy," or "friend," a stuffed toy can be cared for and nurtured.

If your child is upset because you have to leave home or the child-care center, or as the result of another difficult transition that must be made, a stuffed animal is still a comfort, just as when he was a toddler.

You might consider a stuffed animal for yourself, too, as a liaison between you and your little boy's soft toy, or simply for your own pleasure. Buy one or a few for yourself. After all, why should children

**PLAY POINT:** Buy selectively and only what your child really needs. He will have a chance to play with more diversified objects at nursery school and with friends, so it's not necessary to have everything at home. A few simple basics and the child's imagination are quite enough.

be the only ones to enjoy stuffed animals? Many collectors of teddy bears enjoy special events throughout the year like teas and birthday parties.

You can get these cuddly toys in all styles from simple to exotic and complex. There's enough variety to fill Noah's entire ark, so be selective. Your child can play with them in small groups, lining them up for different play situations.

Seek out the stuffed toy that is carefully designed, well-made, and inspected before being distributed, so you can be assured it is safe. Be sure the eyes are permanent and well-fastened, and that other parts cannot fall off or be pulled out.

Stuffed animals can be obtained through Applause, BRIO, Commonwealth, Cultural Toys, Fisher-Price, Folkmanis, GUND, Hasbro, Manhattan Toy, North American Bear Company, PlaySkool, and Steiff. $5–$25.

## 14. Transportation Toys

Children never seem to tire of pushing boats, cars, trains, or trucks around on the floor, tables, or outdoors, while creating appropriate sound accompaniment. This is a significant part of peer play. As your youngster plays, she takes on different personalities: locomotive engineer, airplane pilot, truck driver. She develops her own realistic sounds and dialogue from what she has heard. Children learn a great deal from the roles they portray with their transportation toys.

Dad or mom may want to start collecting trains, parts, and tracks for the offspring who seems to be truly fascinated by them. These are popular collectors' items, and a hobby you and your child can relish. Try to visit a train museum or take a trip on a train. A great experience. You can also find videotapes that portray trains of all kinds and that will fuel your child's imagination and understanding of how trains work.

When you buy transportation toys be sure they are what the child wants and that all the parts work. Children seem to learn early on what is the most popular vehicle and will be influenced by their peers. Do not fight this; it is inevitable—just be on the lookout for quality control.

Look for vehicles by BRIO, Ertl, Galoob, Hasbro, Matchbox, Mattel, Tonka, and Tyco. $4–$20.

## 15. Tricycles

Her first tricycle is a thrill for any young child. As she becomes adept she will want to extend her travels: Be sure she has learned to stop and start the tricycle, knows how to handle herself and her trike as she rides, and see that she rides in safe areas. Teach her courtesy and consideration to other children (even, perhaps especially, if they do not reciprocate).

Your child may want a tricycle with a picture of his favorite television character on it, as he and his peers are often greatly influenced by television advertising. You must decide on the items your child plays with, and this is a good age to teach your child some alternatives to "TV" marketing. Children have the same amount of fun on undecorated tricycles; while the TV promo is good for perhaps two minutes of your child's attention, it does not make for a better ride. Use your own judgment.

In any case, compare prices and quality, as you will want a bike with sturdy construction, one that can stand up to a lot of use.

Companies that make tricycles include Angeles, Fisher-Price, Radio Flyer, and Roadmaster. $25–$50.

## DR. TOY'S TIPS FOR PARENTS OF PRESCHOOLERS

- ❑ Create play clothes and prop boxes including hats, gloves, and shoes for dramatic play.
- ❑ Create opportunities for your child to use large muscles in climbing, crawling, pushing, pulling, jumping, and throwing.
- ❑ Create an art-supply box (used and recycled cards, magazines, and other objects to cut and paste).
- ❑ Create opportunities for the child to attend peer group activities, child care, or regular play groups.
- ❑ Save assorted boxes which can be used for storage, play houses, or climbing.

ADDITIONAL SUGGESTED TOYS FOR PRESCHOOLERS:

Blackboard and chalk

Bowling pins and ball

Bubble pipe

Candy Land game (a basic first game)

Cards (colors, shapes)

Cash register (for play store)

Dressing dolls, play clothes, hats, shoes, and other accessories

Funnel Tunnel (long fabric tunnel)

Jump rope

Kaleidoscopes (great for indoors, outdoors, and travel)

Lacing cards

Large and different-sized cartons (allows the child to use imagination to transform the box into whatever desired)

Magnetic letters for refrigerator

Pegs and Peg-Boards

Picture lotto

Pinwheels

Ring-toss game

Rocking animal

Shapetacktoe (shapes to fit)

Teach-a-Time Clock

Telephone

Tent, covered bridge table, or tepee

Tool kit

Trains

Trampoline

View-Master

Wagon

## ▶ SUMMARY OF PRESCHOOLER DEVELOPMENT

# THREE YEARS

## Physical

- Nimble; climbs, runs, turns well, swings arms.
- Feeds self well.
- Holds cup by handle.
- Tips head back to get last drop.
- Can brush teeth.
- Has full set of temporary teeth.
- Restless sleep.
- Interest in own body.
- Dresses and undresses if helped with buttons.
- Dresses without help depending upon mood.
- Puts on shoes.

## Emotional/Social

- Begins to show some self-control.
- Can make simple choices.
- Tries to please and conform.
- Temper tantrums may occur.
- Imaginary worries; may fear dark, dogs, death.
- Curiosity level rises rapidly.
- Frustrated with obstacles.
- Enjoys praise.
- Responsive to verbal guidance.
- Likes to run errands.
- Loves to be with other children.
- Distinguishes between girls and boys

## Mental

- Knows night from day.
- Can count to five, maybe ten, but can't understand numbers.
- Draws a man on request.
- Has good eye muscles.
- Can copy a circle, cross, or other simple outline.
- May "read" from pictures in book.
- Speaks in sentences and uses pronouns.
- Loves to talk.
- Uses plurals, past tense, personal pronouns, prepositions.
- Knows last name, sex, street on which she lives.
- Remembers simple rhymes.
- Curious; asks "What?" "Where?" "When?"
- Understands simple explanations.
- Asks frequent questions to which he knows answers.
- Likes to learn new words.
- Likes to compare two objects.
- Is vague about time and space.
- Average attention span about ten minutes.
- Sees forms; knows circles, triangles, and squares.
- Can make choice and abide by it.
- Asks for help if needed.
- May not be able to do two things at once, i.e., talk and eat.
- Knows when she's hungry and expresses need.

## At Play

- Rides a tricycle easily.
- Playmates main source of anger response.
- Parallel play with some cooperation.
- Begins to "wait his turn."
- Sings simple songs, not always on pitch.
- Is responsive to rhythm.
- Can throw a ball without losing balance.

- May still play alone quite happily.
- Can make planes, trains, and cars with block play.
- Can recognize familiar melodies.
- Uses slides, climbs, turns sharp corners, digs.
- Can gallop, jump, and run to music.
- Likes paint, crayons, and clay.
- Uses varied and rhythmical strokes in painting and drawing.
- Likes to have picture or artwork saved.
- Beginning to share.
- Can adjust to taking turns.
- Enjoys playmates.
- No sex preference in play.
- Begins to combine things such as pots and dish, bear and cup, sock and shoes.

# FOUR YEARS
## Physical
- Can lace shoes.
- Can stand on one foot, skip on one foot, and then hop on the other.
- Very active: uses shovels, sweeps, rakes, races up and down stairs.
- Can carry liquids without spilling.
- Manages own clothes if they are simple; buttons and unbuttons.

## Emotional/Social
- Episodes of uncontrolled aggression.
- Love of opposite-sexed parent grows.
- Language added to tantrums; name-calling.
- Acts out if she does not get own way.
- Defies parents, but often quotes them as authorities.
- Boastful; dogmatic; bossy.
- Not as sensitive to praise of others.

- Moralistic judgments begin.
- Feels independence and often asserts it.
- Uses swearing and silly words.
- Loves an audience and talks to self or imaginary playmate if none available.
- Total confidence in his own ability to do anything.
- May have an imaginary friend.
- Emotions at surface.
- Sometimes defies adults by hitting, throwing, running away, biting, etc.
- Tests own power.
- Nonconforming, resists routines.
- Senses differences in gaps of skill and powers of adults and self.
- Wants reassurance of being a strong, skillful, capable person.
- Shows little politeness at times.
- Shows off and acts very badly before company if not guided firmly.
- Likes to play mother or teacher to smaller child.
- Shows pride in mother, though may resist her authority.
- Boasts about daddy.

## Mental

- May identify primary colors.
- Can usually count fingers.
- Perceives simple analogies and reasons.
- Begins to abstract, conceptualize, and generalize.
- Some difficulty in separating fact from fancy.
- Concern for origin of babies and death.
- Runs topics into the ground.
- Imagination vivid, rapid, varied.
- Rationalizes own behavior.
- Uses sentences.
- Exaggerates to practice words.

- Tries out silly words and sounds.
- Experiments with adjectives.
- Speaks of imaginary conditions.
- Can tell a lengthy story mixing fact and fancy.
- Asks many questions, not always interested in answers (attention-getting).
- Interested in how answer fits into thought.
- Attention span of twelve to fifteen minutes.
- Can anticipate a tour or trip and help with preparations.
- Talks about trip afterward and reproduces experiences.
- Likes collecting: leaves, pictures, postcards, toys.

## At Play

- Skips and does stunts.
- Climbs well and slides.
- Can cut with scissors on a line.
- Can throw overhand and underhand.
- Holds brush in adult manner.
- Paints in flourishes with running commentary.
- Begins cooperative play, but more content in small group; rapid changes in friends.
- Imaginative, enjoys dramatic play.
- Interested in other children and their activities.
- Capable of group planning and play.
- Can amuse herself alone.
- Play reaches new heights of inventiveness and grows rich in detail.
- Likes to act out ideas.
- Builds elaborate structures and names them.
- Dolls are important, sharing experiences and having personalities.
- Likes to create hazards and does not like to be reminded of limitations.
- Needs guidance and lots of materials.

- Physically aggressive: hits, kicks, throws, and bites; is rough and careless with toys.
- Verbally aggressive.
- Laughs wildly in play.
- Name calling, or bragging with silliness, at times leading to tears and squabbling.
- Is able to accept turns and may share graciously.
- Accepts rules and responds well to objective commands such as "It is time to . . ."
- Has a great interest in music: in listening, dancing, or performing to it.
- Increased control of voice which allows him to sing on pitch.
- Dresses and undresses dolls.
- Works with precision in painting, but shifts ideas.
- Begins to copy pictures and color them in.
- Watches to learn.
- Shows dramatic ability; is beginning to use talking instead of hitting in play.
- Loves story time and enjoys turning pages.
- Enjoys exaggeration, bubbling humor.
- Interest in new experiences, in how and why.
- Loves to talk about things of which the story reminds her.

# FIVE

# Primary Schooler

## BETWEEN FIVE AND EIGHT YEARS OLD

Your child approaches a major milestone in his development when he begins kindergarten. New friends and adventures enlarge his world, and now, as your child grows more independent, the groundwork established by his Play Tutor will govern how well he adjusts.

### Brave New Worlds to Conquer

The primary-school youngster thrives on play groups with new acquaintances. Playthings become more complex and diversified. Many of the products your little one played with last year will continue to hold her attention, but her play experiences are far more varied and complex. Let her make more decisions in choosing her playthings but don't give up your guidance; it continues to be vital, just more indirect.

Each child is unique; each has his own characteristic way of absorbing information and of honing skills. "Individual differences" is the key phrase for the competent teacher, and you, your child's Play Tutor, must assimilate the concept, too. Your son's style of learning will be different from that of the child who sits across the room.

Some children, for example, like figuring things out for themselves (called "trial and error," or heuristic learning) which sets a pattern for a successful Socratic method later: i.e., teacher/Play Tutor–generated questions which elicit discovery response. This is an inductive process. Other children prefer to be shown a procedure and then allowed to practice it: deductive learning. Both styles are used by all of us to grasp new facts and concepts, but each of us responds slightly better to one or the other, depending upon our individual makeup. And each style is more effective in some kinds of problem-solving than in others.

## Playing the Game

During this time, a child plays more games that utilize her large muscles like jumping rope, skating, and two-wheeler bike riding. Your little girl also has greater control over her small muscles, so she can draw, sew, and work puzzles that have lesser-sized and more numerous pieces.

Your family's eager youngster is able to sit still longer and become focused on an activity. He can concentrate on reading and can remain involved with math and science operations. He will explore hobbies and schemes that might stay with him for the rest of his life, and so he should be exposed to the arts, to crafts, to collecting, and to stories of historic eras. Take him to museums, exhibitions of paintings and artifacts, and different special events.

## Play Tutors Play, Too!

Barbara was a single mom by the time her son, Andy, entered first grade and the after-school center. She felt he was making good adjustments to many changes, but she still felt guilty about being a working mother.

To compensate, she picked up extra toys often during lunch

hours, but found Andy did not play with any very long. She wondered why and came to me.

I proposed that she stop feeling guilty as nothing was to be gained by that energy drain, and more, there really wasn't anything she could do at that time to change their circumstances. It was clear to me, moreover, that the excessive toys were overloading Andy. I suggested that instead of making more purchases, she spend more time on weekends playing with her son. This time out to play together was especially important since Andy's father had moved to another state.

The trips Barbara and Andy made to local places of interest vastly improved when Barbara followed another of my ideas and teamed up with a single man she knew and liked. The "boys" became buddies; they found games to play, told each other fine things about the museum displays, and created travel games for the longer trips to places like the Monterey Aquarium.

Now Barbara gets Andy only the things he wants, which he frequently decides upon with the help of his new playmate, who cheerfully takes over some playtime to share.

## Peers Are Here, Peers Are There; Peers It Seems Are Everywhere!

Peer-group acceptance becomes an imperative to your child now. She will tend to find certain special friends that she can "belong to," but at the same time, it has become important to her to relate to groups and group activities.

Your primary grader may feel compelled to conform to his peer group's tastes, including taste in toys. You must decide, however, based on *your* judgment and budget, about the toys you buy. Just because friend "Jaime or Janey has one" doesn't mean you have to buy the same thing. However, get at least one "popular" choice so your child doesn't feel left out of the peer group. You must explain, though, that he should not expect more clones of friends' possessions.

Because children at this age often form close attachments to one or two "bosom pals" and exclude other children, it's time to teach yours not to offend the outsiders with "secrets," and to refrain from being mean: cruel teasing, mocking, name-calling. Show the importance of getting along with all the youngsters.

Your child is ready for learning responsibility, especially about her place in family activities and her contributions to them. Involve her in household tasks, and teach her to take initiative in getting along with people. There will be no better time to instill these values. She is eager to learn, to emulate, and to win approval.

## The Emergence of Self

This is a period of self-conceptualizing. Your young one will examine his appearance and will look for approval from you and others. Mild narcissism is perfectly normal (if not overdone). Your little girl's ability to dress well aids her positive self-image and gives her confidence.

Role-playing at this stage consists of feigning real life experiences. Boys and girls want props that relate to specific places. They like producing impromptu theatrical productions, dressing up in costumes, face painting, and creating disguises. But they are also eager to experience real things, to learn to cook, to sew, or to build a bird feeder or lapboard.

## Let the Games Begin

Children need positive and relaxing alternatives to the intense mental focus of schoolwork. After-school physical activities—large-muscle builders like baseball, basketball, and skating—and creative play—drawing, journal-keeping, practicing guitar—are strongly recommended.

## The Extracurricular Gambits

Take your child to the zoo, the aquarium, the planetarium; to city, state, and national parks; into the country to farms or wildlife preserves. Children need a balance to urban living: encountering animals in their native habitats; seeing the heavens and stars "up close"; discovering the petrification of forests in the southwest; experiencing, if at all possible, an ancient culture like the Anasazi (cliff dwellers of the Pueblo culture who flourished between A.D. 100–1300 in the plateau regions of northern Arizona, New Mexico, and southern Utah and Colorado).

## THE FIVE-YEAR-OLD

At five, children are growing more slowly. Your child needs frequent rest periods because he'll tend to overexert himself. At the same time, though, he may be quieter in his demeanor and seem reluctant to reveal his feelings.

Your youngster should be able to dress and undress herself easily without help except for pesky buttons and bows, or shoelaces and belts. Teach her to get clothes ready the night before; it will reduce stress in the morning. There is a direct corollary to your daughter's smart play with dolls, dressing and undressing them: her skill in doing the same for herself.

### The Family Read

Don't forget to read stories and if you have not already done so, start making read-aloud a family thing and, when possible, a daily ritual (or at least several times a week). This has several pluses. First, as already discussed, you will hook your

> **PLAY POINT:**
> Next to being read to, the single best activity for improving reading, *anyone's*, is reading out loud.

child and her siblings (older *or* younger) on books by igniting a craving to know "what happens next."

Second, let family members take turns as reader, including *all* the adults present and *all* the children present, from the readers of primers to your young college-age person.

A family member or two takes a turn in an evening, and each reads from a group-voted selection, or from his own current favorite. The total session should be about fifteen minutes max (unless there is an outcry for more—and there often will be when an especially good story captivates your audience). Make allowances for varied attention spans: a primary-school child's turn should not exceed one to two minutes.

*This* ritual, replacing TV, is *guaranteed* to raise the IQs and PQs of everyone involved. If the time for the family read (usually just after dinner is best) conflicts with any pet TV show, tape it to watch later. Moreover, it's a *family* bonding time, and an irreplaceable one at that. Don't hesitate to adapt these suggestions to your own preferences.

Make up stories for your youngest—ongoing sagas with nightly cliff-hangers work well—and let your child(ren) have a turn at developing the story. Write down sentences your child makes up.

## The Right Stuff

This is an age to introduce simple scientific and natural materials like magnets, stethoscopes, and magnifying glasses, especially when found in a favorite story, like a family read of H. G. Wells. Your youngster, if he has not already done so, will become interested in the clock and telling time. Show her the difference between digital and analog. She'll want to know about weighing scales and your explanation about what you are doing, and why, when you weigh out food at the store, or determine the weight of letters and packages for mailing.

Many play activities your child has been embarked upon for some time become more complex as his skills increase. Beads are now easier to string and he can do more complicated craft and art activities. Complex block and fitted-piece constructions have become possible, as have smaller-pieced puzzles and intricate drawing.

# THE SIX-YEAR-OLD

A six-year-old is in an active period between that of the quiet five-year-old and restrained seven-year-old. Your young explorer is now more capable, more skilled, and more responsible; he is also more stubborn and opinionated. He becomes the center of his own universe and he is seriously involved in that Very Important Person: himself. Many children, and perhaps yours, tend to be defiant and won't listen to directions. It is essential for you to understand such phases of development when they appear and to keep your sense of balance. And, especially, to bite more than a few bullets of patience.

The fact is, children of five, six, and seven have developed insecurities, a by-product of the enormous number of new milieus in which they find themselves. They are afraid to make mistakes and are quite sensitive. Your positive guidance and support will help considerably.

On the bright side, they are also tremendously curious, ask lots of questions, and are eager to learn. Many still come to mom and dad for cuddles, hugs, and other signs of affection.

This is a fine time for them to develop musical, writing, dancing, or art skills. See that your offspring has a chance to find her individual gifts, and if you see that she is seriously interested in one of more of the arts, find her a reputable coach or trainer and time for practice.

Imaginative play with books, games, and experiments should be encouraged. You can reinforce the skills he is learning at school by having him read aloud to you at home, guiding him toward hobby projects, and enlivening his interests in science, nature, and biology. Find time to take walks; exercise with him, and invite him to make things with you.

# THE SEVEN-YEAR-OLD

Your first- or second-grader is apt to be a perfectionist and do tasks over and over. She totally involves herself in favorite play projects. She will likely compete with siblings and other children; her peer group is very influential in what she thinks she wants and thinks she needs. Your little girl and her friends like action games and acting out group dramas and fantasies.

But this age also introduces the joys of aloneness—independent play, doing things by herself. She'll alternate naturally between inside play and outside play.

A definite separation takes place now between the boys and the girls as they regard each other with ambivalence and apparent dislike (which may not be dislike at all!). Whether boy or girl, the types of activities with friends change. Building elaborate structures such as a playhouse, treehouse, or clubhouse is pursued with best friends.

Primary-school children—six-, seven-, and eight-year-olds—will often not take well to peer teasing, and feistiness may appear suddenly in your heretofore placid child. He simply will not like to be picked on, and if he does not develop his own defense mechanisms, mom and dad must provide comfort, reassurance, and quite important, sensible advice on how to protect himself. Now is *not* the time to tell him to "be a good sport." No child of any age should be expected to endure cruelty. Instead, give him the classic tips for dealing with uncivilized behavior, whether temper tantrums or insults: firmly changing the subject, making a joke of it, and/or (if your youngster shows an aptitude for this) turning the verbal tables with subtlety and wit. This is an instance where the reading habit your family established aids him to be articulate and more clever than the poor souls who may have so little of those qualities available to them.

Eight

# THE EIGHT-YEAR-OLD

This period introduces a physical turning point for your child, which shows in his increasing body coordination, sense of rhythm, and hand/eye synchronization. Games involving small-muscle integration attract him. Reading and writing achievement seem to escalate. He will be intrigued by specific products which help him write and create books. He might try to move faster to complete a project than is possible for him, and then he'll make mistakes and become frustrated. His Play Tutor can ameliorate such frustrations by suggesting an alternate method to try, or by introducing an easier plaything.

Obtain well-crafted figures for fantasy and models, because she can now appreciate such quality. Provide puppets, books, and materials she can use for dramatic play.

She may enjoy manipulating math materials like Cuisenaire rods. Many children love to use play money, clocks that teach time-telling (although in some children this starts a few years earlier), and learning an abacus. Science sets which deal with weather, plants, and animals usually fascinate her.

If you like gardening, show your child how to plant seeds and how to create simple gardens. Correlate science sets with trips to science museums. The eight-year-old is ready for elementary anatomy, astronomy, and computer work.

Your child can enjoy games without major emphasis on competition, but for most children eight is an age when calculation, strategy, and frankly, winning are paramount. A lengthening attention span leads to self-directed play, and activity kits challenge him and keep his interest.

Your young boy or girl will try acrobatics, climbing, and gymnastics. Bike-riding begins to take on show-time characteristics in simulating eleven- and twelve-year-old brothers who are adept at wheelies and jumping curbs. Don't panic at falls and scrapes. This is Experiment with What My Bod Can Do time. There are trees to climb and brother's skateboards and in-line skates to try out (with inevitable comment about this from brother), and eight is not too young to purchase either item. Just provide plenty of supervision from yourself or older sibling, if brother is reliable. East and West Coast kids will start riding on skateboards.

Your child's Play Tutor comes into strong evidence now. Make it attractive to her to include you in such activities to give pointers and safety tips (and a lot of not-obvious supervision!). Activities like these continue to enrich your child's Play Quotient and maintain your loving, happy relationship.

## TOY SUGGESTIONS FOR FIVE- TO EIGHT-YEAR-OLDS

| | | |
|---|---|---|
| 1. | Art supplies | (C) |
| 2. | Bicycles | (A) |
| 3. | Books | (E) |
| 4. | Construction toys | (E) |
| 5. | Dolls, dollhouses, figures, toy soldiers | (E) |
| 6. | Electronic games | (E) |
| 7. | Jump ropes | (E) |
| 8. | Kites | (A) |
| 9. | Musical instruments | (A) |
| 10. | Nonelectronic games | (C) |
| 11. | Puppets and marionettes | (C) |
| 12. | Puzzles | (E) |
| 13. | Software | (E) |
| 14. | Tools | (A) |
| 15. | Transportation toys | (E) |

## 1. Art Supplies

The child-development term *maturation* carries with it an implication beyond that of the simple maturing process. It describes an unfolding where an ability typical of an earlier age evolves in a complex and elaborate manner.

This seems particularly true of talent, like creating good artwork. (Parenthetically, the talented person typically is gifted in all the arts: drawing and painting, music and singing, creative writing. The great artists usually have simply chosen one talent to study and develop to a high degree and could have done so with any of their other aptitudes.) As resident Play Tutor for your child, a very important job is to identify her talents—and all of us have one or two, sometimes never discovered! The Play Tutor works to put his child in touch with those talents, see which appeal most to her, then supplies the support and materials to let the youngster take off!

At the same time, never, *never* push your child in a direction which may not be his—which may, more likely, be one of yours! And one you may have neglected. Give him ideals, give him love, and give him freedom to seek his own course.

Sketching, painting, modeling clay, woodworking, sewing or embroidery, needlework (cross-stitch, petit point, plastic canvas projects, or knitting), wood or linoleum engraving, leather work, model building, beadwork, photography—these are all arts in which your child might find a special interest. Other projects can include weaving with a loom, jewelry making, papier-mâché, creations, model trains, and throwing pottery.

Starting young is as important in art expression as in musical training. Once a child discovers the exhilaration of creating something uniquely her own, she will want to continue. Display her work. Make a place where she can work without interfering with anyone else—or being interfered with!

Your youngster's art helps him amplify his sensory awareness and develop a sense of color, shape, and form. When you see he has not only the interest, but a gift for drawing (get an outside-family opinion!), schedule your trips to art museums and galleries with an eye to helping him understand where he's going and what he can do if he chooses to work hard.

Art supplies are available from art-supply stores and some toy stores. Makers of supplies include ALEX, Avalon (stitchery, latch hook), Binney & Smith (color supplies), Children's Out of School Time, Creativity Kits, Fisher-Price, Galt Toys (easels, supplies), and Rose Art. $2–$10.

## 2. Bicycles

The first bike. There's not much that will bring more joy and excitement to your youngster than this. Make it a special occasion. Network to discover the local bike store which will help you make a good selection.

The involvement of both parents is desirable now, for helping your little boy or girl learn to balance on the two-wheeler. Teaching safety and how to ride properly is easier with two mentors. See that he likes and wears his helmet. He can even decorate it with stickers to make it individual, but it is important to teach safety and proper use of bike and helmet.

Riding bicycles has a multitude of advantages. It increases physical dexterity, motor skills, confidence, and independence. It's an entry to the brotherhood (or sisterhood) of your child's friends. The sense of being "one of the gang" makes her feel good about herself. It gives her mobility, gets her to school, to friends' houses, and helps her run (safe) errands for mom or dad.

A schoolteacher friend of mine with four children (ranging in age from two and a half to sixteen years old) and her husband made weekly treks out of their urban neighborhood to the neighboring state park just north of San Francisco. The low traffic roads meandered through some of the loveliest country in Northern California.

Jim, with the boys' help, made the rack that fit on top of their van. Five bikes, upside-down on the rack, drew stares and toots when they drove along the road.

The toddler's seat was on dad's bike; the picnic basket on mom's. Teenage son carried the beverage hamper. The nine-year-old raced along and the thirteen-year-old, on her pink-and-white confection, rode sedately, stopping to make friends with curious horses in their white-fence corrals. To this day, with all the kids grown, they have a remarkably close family relationship. The boys call their mom for *advice* (which never ceases to amaze her since they never listened when they were in their teens). "Ah, well," she says. "Guess I'm like Mark Twain. I seem to have learned a whole bunch since then, though it took almost twenty years to do it!"

Consider family bike outings and treks. These are great experiences for the whole family to share.

Bicycles are produced by Fuji, Hedstrom, Huffy, Radio Flyer, Roadmaster, Schwinn, and Sears. $50–$200.

## 3. Books

Play Tutors help their child establish good reading habits. But keep building on it (it never stops, you know, not until she's moved out on her own and even then you'll be comparing notes on books you've read).

Talk to your child's teacher, to your local librarian, to the County Educational Resource Center and request book lists or-

> **PLAY POINT:** Let your child begin to build her personal library. In the case of library books she especially likes, purchase personal copies for her. Many wonderful paperbacks are available with a wide range of interests and themes.

ganized by reading grade level. Select books from these lists to buy or to check out of the library. Haunt used-book stores. If you've followed my recommendations at his earlier ages you may see that by eight years old your son will be reading at the fourth- and fifth-grade reading levels.

In addition to introducing more sophisticated books, you might encourage your youngster to keep a Book Log: tracking the books she reads, perhaps grading them, whether keepers or sellers (yes, you can resell books to used-book stores), and perhaps a comment or two about the book. Some children might like to know the date they finished the book, too, how long it was, and/or how long it took to read.

A Book Log is handy for preventing the purchase of duplicates (a problem for the voracious reader!). It's the kind of activity that encourages building a collection—her own library—too.

Now is the time for a most important step in your child's development. You have read aloud to him and in the supportive family circle he has been encouraged to take a turn reading from his school primer. Now, if you want your child to be an above-average reader, to raise, literally, his IQ, it is time for the next step in acquiring that proficiency. It requires two things: He *must* read *aloud* to you every day, and you must be very patient with his stumbles and prompt only when absolutely necessary. By the age of eight, schedule two five-minute "read-alouds" to hear him, separated by at least an hour (other homework? an approved TV show?) so he won't get too tired. At least one of these read-aloud times should be over and above the family read. Also he will be reading directions on craft or hobby kits, games, and software.

Trips to the library should be part of his regular schedule, and maintaining a library card is a very good idea. Children enjoy story hours and other such activities set up by the library staff. Watch for book sales by the "Friends of the Library" or other sources, as a good way to add to your child's home collection.

While helping your child build her reading habit, it is a natural corollary to encourage her writing skills. She should be learning the tools of grammar at school now (and if she's not, change schools!), and so, at home, discover what kind of writing she likes to do—describing a process, reporting an event, creating a story, composing a poem—and not only encourage her to write but give her *honest* critiquing. Do not praise something that isn't really wonderful. The real world won't. Use the good teacher's formula:

1. Tell what's good about the creation.
2. Identify specifically the things that need work and supply tips on how to do it.
3. Then tell her again what's good about her work.

And do read her original stories out loud. Keep them in a folder and date them. These efforts will be treasured over the years along with the artwork selectively saved.

Writing longhand should be easier for the eight-year-old now (and teacher should be teaching good penmanship) but consider checking out a keyboarding class for your child's age level and sign him up. You'll do him no favors if you allow him to hunt and peck on your computer (slows him down and keeps him slow; makes learning the touch method later tremendously more difficult), and typing gaffes will make his publishers unhappy when he produces his first best-seller. Keyboarding allows him to use typewriter or computer. Besides the standard formatting and conventions of typing, it will also teach punctuation, spelling, syllable division, and a sense of grammar and syntax.

Books are published by Bobbs-Merrill; Delacourte; Doubleday; EDC; HarperCollins; Knopf; Little, Brown; McGraw-Hill; Penguin; Random House; Scholastic; and Simon & Schuster. $2–$10.

## 4. Construction Toys

These sets continue to refine hand/eye coordination, and the ones for this age level are challenging. They lend themselves well to children working together. Often these toys accumulate and you may think your child has enough to start a small company. Good storage will be necessary, or weeding out and giving away is an option.

At this stage your child will be drawn to making complicated structures and her new structures will stay up longer. Some sets provide for attaching motors.

Fine-motor dexterity is enhanced by working these sets, and her imagination takes off. Spatial proportions, understanding of sequences, and following directions are reinforced.

The child will find many possibilities in materials like Erector sets, KAPLA, K'NEX, Learning Curve Robotix, Learning Materials Workshop, LEGO SYSTEMS, Playmobil, Rokenbok, and Tinkertoys. $5–$25.

## 5. Dolls, Dollhouses, Figures, Toy Soldiers

As girls get older, their interest in dolls, doll accessories, and doll-houses becomes quite sophisticated. At this age, starting a collection begins to be of interest.

Dolls provide role-playing activities like those when your child was younger, but the stories and events are far more worldly. She will become more interested in specific types of dolls, like adult fashion mannequins. Your daughter may wish to create a doll to fit different places or scenes such as a farm, scenes from the past, those in nature—skiing, training horses—or scenes that are pure fantasy—such as finding a treasure in a splendid castle. Dolls come in all costumes for all purposes.

Your daughter may want to complete a dollhouse. The number of dollhouses, furnishings, miniatures, and accessories to choose from is outstanding. Many come ready-made, or you can make them yourself. Selectivity is important, otherwise your child's room can begin looking like a crowded doll convention. Encourage your child to care for the dolls and the dollhouse and keep them in good condition.

Consider including multicultural dolls for your child regardless of her ethnicity. This teaches respect for one's own and others' heritages and cultivates her sense of worth and identity.

Toy soldiers, presented by the involved and informed parent, need not teach warlike standards. On the contrary, they can be used to teach the futility of war when you explain the reasons and results of each battle, especially if told as an interesting story, like the tales of Waterloo, the taking of Washington, D.C., during the War of 1812, the Battle of Hastings in 1066, and even Julius Caesar's crossing of the Rubicon. (This is for the parent or uncle who enjoys a little research.) Action figures mesh with recent movies or TV shows that become popular and interest in collecting the many objects that are made to promote or support the film is high. You will have to decide how much of this stuff you want to invest in or at all. I have some questions about the efficacy of action figures. These little but pricey items become valuable collectibles among the peer group and it becomes a status symbol to have the latest fad.

Some companies to look for when selecting dolls are Alexander Doll, American Girl, Corolle, Effanbee, Fanny's Playhouse, Fisher-Price, Goetz Dolls, Mattel, Olmec, and Uneeda.

Action figures and toy soldiers are available from Galoob, Hasbro, and Mattel. Britains makes the most detailed toy soldiers, which are popular collectibles. $8–$35.

Dollhouses are available from Dolls and Dreams, Fisher-Price, Greenleaf Products, Hasbro, and Little Tikes. $25–$125. You may also obtain more information about dollhouses and furnishings to build from the Miniatures Industry Association of America (614-452-4541 or on the Web at: http://www.creative-industries.com/miaa).

## 6. Electronic Games

Although the joystick computer games (like Nintendo) are innovations that are very big right now, I believe they are of limited long-range play value. My objections are that they become excessively used because of the novelty and, for some children, the games become terribly boring or, worse, hypnotic to the point of fogging original thought and creativity. After a while the child learns the key to the game, and it shortly gets monotonous. Then she'll want a new game that has more figures, more noise, and more action—this can get very, very expensive.

Despite the excitement and innovation of joysticks and Super

Mario Bros., children find that gobbling up opponents soon loses its appeal. Children, like adults, are turned off by "same old, same old. . . ." We should be wary of technological fads that do not teach positive values to children. More noncompetitive games allow children to learn something and still have fun. Don't overlook games that offer challenge, have staying power, and require individual ingenuity.

> **PLAY POINT:** **Limit the amount of time spent in electronic-game activity. Encourage a diversity of other activities and interests and do not allow lopsidedness in any area, even beneficial ones. Balance of activities helps your child turn to balanced interests. While electronic games and computer software can give the child learning experiences, not all contribute to healthy, positive development. Avoid violent programming.**

Not all electronic games are actually bad. But most are too often mind-limiting, eye-straining, and frequently teach skewed values like excessive violence. It is doubtful the "skills" learned add to intelligence, creativity, or emotional growth.

Children want them because they are a fast-moving, popular trend, and of course, best-buddy Jaime has one. It is, however, better to limit the amount of time spent on the game (have Jaime over to your place as much as you can where the Play Tutor may—subtly—influence the gaming!).

The military games may be useful for military procedures but ask yourself how applicable they are; can you relate them to real-life experiences? Do you want to?

I know children play with electronic games because they are a trend, and it's very hard to resist trends. However, do limit the time, or the electronics will divert attention from Smart Play.

Suggested electronic games are sports games like basketball, hockey, soccer, baseball, and football; Odyssey, and Super Simon. $25–$150.

## 7. Jump Ropes

This is a classic used by little children and grown-up athletes for generations. Some of the jump-rope games, like "Over the Stream—Under the Stream," have been around for years. If your child skips rope at this age with friends, she improves social development and also learns the techniques of rope jumping early enough to ensure proficiency as she grows older.

Taking turns is a primary part of jump rope. Physically, your child develops coordination, muscular strength, rhythm, and timing. You could try it, too (to see if you can still jump as you used to!). It's fun for your child and exercise for you—and vice versa!

Jump ropes are made by Skokum. $2–$5.

## 8. Kites

What mystery and fascination kites hold for children! They feel a sense of power and mastery when they make the kite swoop and dive in the wind. Flying a kite is a chance to play with dad and mom and gives kids a great opportunity to learn a little science as well. Flying kites is an active outdoor sport; it also teaches about air currents and aerodynamics, not as a dry subject, but by hands-on experience. Your child acquires balance and learns the remarkable sensory awareness we see when they run gracefully and easily around the park, eyes only on the kite, and somehow avoid obstacles on the ground.

Kites today are a far cry from the paper and crisscross balsa wood that most of us were familiar with when we were growing up. (The old standbys exist, but there are just a lot more designs to choose from.) Some make outstanding room decorations on the days when it's not windy enough to fly them.

There are special kite stores you can visit, with all of the colors and designs on display, a delight to the eye. Or you might think of making one for or with your youngster and watch the remarkable affair you and she created soar!

Kites can be obtained from Go Fly a Kite, Hi-Flier, and Tide Rider. $5–$20.

## 9. Musical Instruments

It is never too early to start learning music and it helps a child build upon and express his talent and share with friends. One group of children I know created a band with an appropriate name, "Sibling Rivalry," and were widely recognized not only among family and peers, but also at school functions. Some members went on to professional careers in music.

I have recommended that babies hear quiet music tapes early. If your child shows interest and talent, make sure he has good instructors who like teaching children. Regular practice times are essential. You may have to issue some reminders, but if more than that becomes necessary, it is vital never, *ever* to force or coerce a child to practice his music. You can put him off it forever.

If you are tempted to do this, reevaluate whether lessons are really appropriate for your child. If she wants music to be a part of her, to be the best she can be at it, she will play music in preference to other things. If not, then take the pressure off her and refocus toward *listening* appreciation. Don't deny her a music experience just because she dislikes practicing.

If, on the other hand, it is evident that yours is a prodigy who'd rather work on his music than socialize, talk to a child specialist about setting up the right environment for him and guiding him to an appropriate balance that will not harm either his gift or his interest in it.

Musical instruments for children are available from Chicco, Fisher-Price, Hohner, and Yamaha. $5–$25.

## 10. Nonelectronic Games

In this category, nonelectronic games, are those played on table-tops, like board games (Monopoly, checkers, chess, backgammon), and a surprising variety of card games. There are certain games, too, that can be played on the personal computer, like Jeopardy!, poker, and bridge (all obtainable in youth or basic versions), but I do not rank these with dedicated electronic games like Tetris (see page 135–37).

Computer software is different. It can provide action and learning experiences that are much more fun and contribute better to overall development. Some of the sport-games software can provide greater knowledge of how those games are played in real life.

Games like marbles, Ping-Pong, jacks, and hopscotch are fine physical endeavors, and games like Junior Trivial Pursuit, Yahtzee, and Scrabble are excellent mental stimulators. Parlor games like charades combine physical, mental, and social skills.

Games develop the concepts of strategy, logic, and planning, i.e., longer-term goals. They are particularly valuable in improving concentration, both in duration and intensity. Young people like competition, as good teachers have known for decades (spelling bees, Knowledge Bowls, public-speaking and essay contests, and especially the competitive value of grades: GPA as entry to college).

As your child improves his reading skills, he will understand game instructions. Skill development abounds: reading, spelling, guessing, thinking, memorizing, fantasizing. The spirit of adventure, taking (educated) risks, and interacting competitively with others are introduced. Fine-motor skills and coordination are supported by the physical games.

# DR. TOY'S GUIDE TO THE VALUE OF GAMES

❏ Games are an important part of play and growing up.
❏ Games help teach young people strategy, logic, and how to count, read, think ahead, make decisions, cooperate with other people, compete, win gracefully, and lose cheerfully.
❏ Because adults often forget some of these basic lessons, games are important for them, too.
❏ Games reflect life. They can be good "reality therapy."

SUGGESTED GAMES:

*Animal, Vegetable, Mineral*
*Bailiwick*
*Basic Bridge for Kids*
*Big Boggle*
*Careers*
*Checkers*
*Chess*
*Clue*
*Junior Jeopardy!*
*Junior Trivial Pursuit*
*Korombologe*
*Make It Up!*
*Master Mind*

*Moneywise Kids*
*Monopoly*
*Priceless*
*Rat-A-Tat Cat*
*Ring Toss*
*Risk*
*Scrabble*
*SET: The Family Game of Visual Perception*
*Sorry*
*Splash!*
*Survival or Extinction: The Dinosaur Game*
*13 Dead End Drive**

*Thomas the Tank Engine Math Game*
*Ticktacktoe*
*Tutti Frutti*
*25 Words or Less*
*Twister*
*Uno*
*Where in the World Is Carmen Sandiego?*
*Yahtzee*

*Three-dimensional: combines strategy with model building.

# DR. TOY'S CHECKLIST FOR SELECTING GAMES

1. **Is the game challenging?** If the game doesn't make your child think or plan ahead, it may be too easy to win or end too quickly. If the game does not leave some feeling of accomplishment, then an important part is missing.

2. **Is the game too frustrating?** A game that is unbeatable is the same as one that is too easy. No one likes to be discouraged. A game must be carefully designed to give all players a chance.

3. **Is there a reward?** What is the goal of the game? Is there a finish line, a clear-cut point when someone is declared the winner? Playing until the game beats you or until you fail is frustrating, and more, is tiring. Rewards and reinforcement teach; negatives and inevitable losing do not.

4. **Does the game have "repeat-play value"?** A good game won't collect dust in the closet; it should be playable often. Is each round fresh and interesting? Does it challenge and entertain each time it is played?

Games are produced by Aristoplay, Binary Arts, Buffalo Games, Family Games, Gamewright, Koplow Games, Milton Bradley, Parker Brothers, Pressman, University Games, U.S. Games Systems and Voyagers. $5–$35.

## 11. Puppets and Marionettes

If your child has had the opportunity to play with puppets when she was younger, she will expand her earlier dramas and role-playing experiences. Her sets will now be more elaborate and she'll want to try new and different kinds of puppets, and will make up complex dramas and characters for her shows.

At age five, six, seven, and eight, she can usually move handheld puppets quite deftly. If given a chance, many children will delight in marionettes—those complicated string- driven, articulated, and marvelously costumed dolls. And puppets work well for involving older children and siblings to amuse a younger brother or sister. Puppets or marionettes for the older child may become an appealing hobby.

Between the ages of five and eight, children become more able to handle costumes, props, scenery, and background music of their productions. By age eight, your youngster can manipulate marionettes that are jointed. Purchase marionette mannequins so that your child can paint and decorate them especially for the dramas that are a product of her mind. Check some of the many "how to" puppet and marionette publications so that you can provide her guidance in this.

If your child is captivated by making up stories as his puppets talk rapidly and there is a lot of laughter coming from the conversations, you might want to obtain a puppet theatre with a range from very simple to more complex. Select those from Beka, Fisher-Price, and Science Passports. $30–$200.

Puppets are made by Applause, Battat, Eden, Fanny's Playhouse, Folkmanis, GUND, Manhattan Toy, and Steiff. $5–$25.

## 12. Puzzles

A quiet activity, jigsaw puzzles have many variations, including the three-dimensional kind. As the child grows older, he can handle ever larger puzzles with ever smaller pieces. This play strengthens fine-motor dexterity, figure manipulation awareness, a sense of spatial relationships and how things fit together, and gives the feeling of accomplishment and closure.

Puzzles are made by Bepuzzled, Colorforms, DaMert, FX Schmid, Hasbro, Lauri, Milton Bradley, and PlaySkool. $5–$10.

## 13. Software

Money invested in a computer is money wisely spent on the child of today. Every child benefits from some time on the computer.

The time must be monitored and balanced with other hands-on and outdoor activities. The technology of the computer enables the child to learn on an individual level, and with the Internet new doors of learning open wide. Software can teach language, phonics, geography, history, math, provide art experiences, and much more. Computers are usually easy for children to learn to use, and your child will be fascinated with doing so. You can find a good computer in almost every price range. There is a lot of free share-ware available as well as great software titles from many fine companies. Choose your titles carefully. Look at company web sites, *Dr. Toy's Guide*, and magazines to obtain more specific guidance to current, potentially appropriate titles. Many stores will allow trials in the store. If not, read the box carefully before you buy. Check for age grading, names you can trust, recommendations, and suitability of the information provided.

Use your link on the computer for parenting guidance, toy and product information, and much more. See "Dr. Toy's Tips for Selecting Software for children" in Chapter 6, page 161.

Software is available from Broderbund, Davidson, Discovery Channel, Disney Interactive, Edmark, Electronic Arts, Hasbro Interactive, Headbone, Homongous Entertainment, Knowledge Adventures, Learning Company, Living Books, Maxis, MECC, Microsoft, Mindplay, Optimum Resource, Panasonic Interactive, Philips Media, RMC, Sanctuary Woods, 7th Level, Sierra On-Line, Simon & Schuster Interactive, Sunburst Communications, Theatrix, Windy Hill Productions, and many others. $15–35.

## 14. Tools

Why not provide your child with some real tools: a hammer, nails, a set of screwdrivers, rulers, and boards? Child-size kits are available, but children often grow bored with them and they want the real thing. When you are ready to buy, be creative: Look for sales, or go to the five-and-dime, to garage sales, and to flea markets. Choose implements, however, of a size, weight, and shape that are comfortable for her to handle, and won't get in the way of her learning how to use them skillfully.

If you are working on a project, let your youngster help, so he can learn the proper ways to handle tools. It benefits the child (girl or boy) to understand how wood gets cut and how buildings are constructed. A trip to a construction or remodeling site will make the theory you have taught come alive.

Tool kits are available from Little Contractor and Skilcraft. $1–$10.

## 15. Transportation Toys

As your child's world broadens and her perceptions grow, she becomes very aware of the significance transport has in her life. Where once a car was just a car, now a car is a Mustang, Corvette, or Firebird.

Peer pressure is fierce at this age. You may find your child wants to collect H.O. tracks and trains, or a fleet of ship models. These items can be costly and may require you to prioritize. Collections, though, are both playthings and investments and are certainly worth pursuing if your daughter shows a persistent, genuine interest.

One way your son or daughter can start to collect is by your introducing models for him to build. This activity is layered with value: He has the fun of creating a ship, or vintage car, or World War I aeroplane, or horse that the crusader knight mounted, and it will also cut down on the expense of purchasing a manufactured item which, of the replica sort he has built, is very costly. And, most of all, this is something he'll want to keep. When he's in college you may still find yourself batting aside the balsa biplane suspended from the ceiling, so that you can vacuum and dust his room.

Your daughter may be equally intrigued with models. She, like her brother, may need your help in the beginning, but don't do the work for her. Let her feel proud of what she's done, *on her own!* Start with simple models which are easy to assemble and let your child set the pace at which complexity advances.

Remote-control vehicles and planes will draw the interest of the older child, and of course, fathers! Be sure you select a set that is not too complex for him and though parents can (and should) help, don't take over. Nothing frustrates a child more than standing on the sidelines while *his* plane is being assembled by daddy, adjusted by daddy, and flown and maneuvered by daddy—and *not* himself. It's not your little boy's toy anymore and he's likely to reject it entirely. So, if need be, get *two* planes—one for each of them!

Transportation toys help primary schoolers comprehend real-life needs and challenges, whether it is the semi that gets perishable foods from one place to another, the ambulance which transports an accident victim to the hospital, a motorcycle that enables the police officer to chase down a dastardly villain, or the full-size sedan that takes a full size family to a country picnic.

Transportation toys are available from Corgi, Darda, Ertl, Galoob, Lionel, Marklin, Matchbox, and Mattel. $10–$50.

SELECTED TRANSPORTATION TOYS:

- Cars of all sizes and types
- Farm equipment
- Fire engines and emergency vehicles
- Models of cars, knights and their horses, planes, and ships
- Service-station equipment
- Super dump truck
- Train sets

# TOYS AND ACTIVITIES FOR PRIMARY GRADES

- Balls, bats, mitts, face masks, helmets
- Books—all kinds
- Bop Bag (hit the bag—a clown figure—and it returns upright)
- Bulletin board, burlap or cork

- Computer (with word processing to practice keyboarding)
- Crafts
- Dominoes
- Dress-up mirror
- Hobby kits
- Ice skates
- Juggling balls or scarves
- Kaleidoscope
- Lotto
- Microphone (cordless mike for performing)
- Mirror
- Paper dolls
- Play houses
- Play mats
- Role-playing materials
- Sewing cards and embroidery
- Skill-building materials
- Sports
- Stuffed animals
- Tape recorder
- Target games
- Tent/tepee
- Toolbox
- Typewriter (if computer/word processing not available)
- Velcro bat and ball for games
- Video stories
- View-Master (viewer and cards)
- Yo-yos

▶ **DEVELOPMENTAL MILESTONES OF THE PRIMARY SCHOOLER**

# FIVE YEARS

## Physical
- Agile.
- Poised and controlled motor ability.
- Can tie shoelaces.
- Spontaneous drawing with definite ideas in mind; can copy a triangle.
- Knows full name and address.
- Knows primary colors.
- Knows morning from afternoon.
- Girls about one year ahead of boys in growth.
- Handedness well established (between two and five).
- Can tie a bow, but not snugly.

## Emotional/Social
- Wondering about themselves and other people.
- Self-confidence to develop relationships with others.
- Sensitive to ideas, what is said, and conversations.
- Thinks about their own feelings.
- Much self-criticism, but also calm and self-confident.
- Where age four rambles in speech, age five can stop after completing a thought; increase in self-control.
- Does not get lost.
- Calm and self-confident most of the time.
- Likes to finish what he begins and brings projects home with pride.
- Temper tantrums end and courtesy is at a high.
- Strong sense of personal identity.
- Well-adjusted and happy age.
- Individuality and lasting traits appear.

## PLAY POINTS

- **Beginning school does not mean the end of a child's need for play.**
- **Real, fantasy, and play experiences help the learning process. Playing supports and nourishes cognitive, social, and emotional development.**
- **Each child will not demonstrate all potential interests and abilities for his age range. Individual differences pertain to all youngsters. Skills and interests may vary by two years or more. There will be differences in how each child learns, because of her interests and preferences. What is useful for one child may not be so for another.**
- **Culture and past experience increase differences as children grow older. They become more self-conscious as peers influence their play.**
- **Parents must consider their child's background, abilities, interests, emotional maturity, and readiness when evaluating playthings, big toys, books, and other products.**

- Purposeful, constructive.
- Refines emotions.
- Conforms: the "angelic age."
- Well organized.
- Self-contained and responsible.
- Obedient.
- Can now show anger to peer by exclusion rather than physical attack or name-calling.
- Generosity increases.
- Emotions more stable.
- More able to verbalize than display physical emotion.
- Less fear.
- Takes people for granted.
- Mother is center of universe, although has good relationship with daddy.
- Enjoys grandparents' visits.
- Likes time limits; has a sense of order.
- Finds real world enough novelty because has learned what is fantasy and not.
- Likes instruction to improve.
- May be good or a pest with company.
- Sometimes asks permission; may ask many times for the same thing.
- Feels protective toward younger ones.

## Mental

- Learning language quickly.
- Able to communicate and explain feelings and ideas.
- Vocabulary of two thousand well-utilized words.
- Responsive to new ideas and has a lot of imagination.
- Enjoys going from one experience to another.
- Can separate truth from fancy.
- Thoughts are concrete.
- Enjoys going to school.
- Socialized pride in appearance and accomplishments.
- Uses well-defined sentences.
- Likes to count and can count ten objects.
- Answers questions.
- Asks for information, not merely to talk.
- Can carry a plot in a story and repeat a long sequence accurately.
- Interested in why.
- Enjoys repetitive sounds.
- Favorite questions: "How does it work?" "Why is it like that?" "What is it for?"
- Likes models for guides.
- Likes definite task.
- Very good at problem-solving.
- Is not apt to attempt something unless it can be finished.
- Likes concrete results when she has made an effort.
- Thinks before he speaks.
- Is observant, self-critical, self-dependent, proud of work, clothes, etc.
- Is factual, literal, and has remarkable memory.

## At Play

- Has played at home with toys, utensils, furniture, and other items.
- Likes to play house with fantasy.

- Relatively short attention span and enjoys building with blocks, playing with toys.
- Dramatizes life in play with detail.
- Likes group play.
- Likes experience outside the home.
- Fills dramatic play with dialogue and commentary having to do with everyday life.
- Likes realistic props.
- Draws crude but realistic reproductions of scenes.
- Interprets meaning of a picture.
- Can identify missing part of a picture.
- Begins to paint with an idea in mind.
- Finds play is practice for life rather than invention.
- Can ride on scooter.
- Tries to jump rope.
- Wants to discard trike for bike.
- Plays in social group without much conflict—most cooperatively with group of three children.
- Better in outdoor play than indoor.
- Plans surprises and jokes.
- Shows flashes of resistance which are usually quickly overcome.
- Uses verbal aggression.
- Prefers playmates her own age.
- May cry if angry or tired.
- Can march to music.

# SIX YEARS
## Physical
- Active and boisterous.
- Physical growth slows down.
- Large muscles better developed than small.
- Eyes not yet mature; tendency toward farsightedness (some

children not quite ready to read, although children tending to nearsightedness will be able to see words well).
- Permanent teeth begin to appear.
- Heart is in period of rapid growth.

## Emotional/Social
- Ambivalence.
- Has ideas of good and bad.
- Fears remote danger, ridicule, ghosts.
- Tense, upset, unpredictable.
- Shows off; less cooperative than at five.
- Strongly embarrassed by lack of physical privacy.
- Often less mature at home than with outsiders.
- Difficulty making decisions.
- Boys' and girls' interests begin to differ.
- Needs praise, warmth, patience.
- Has a great fear of supernatural and that parents will die.
- Indecisive.
- Independent.
- Beginning social personality.

## Mental
- Can copy a diamond shape.
- Names days of week.
- Knows right from left.
- Counts out any number up to ten, from a grouping of objects.
- Regresses when tired.
- Short interest span.
- Vocabulary over two thousand words in first grade.

## Play
- Likes competition.
- Group play (chaotic).
- Learning competition and cooperation.

- More interest in peer group than family.
- Competent at large-muscle activities including: throwing, jump rope, street games, hopscotch, acrobatics, climbing, skating, bicycle riding, and other sports (water, basketball, softball, football).
- Capable of small-muscle activities, including: painting, printing, drawing, tracing, sewing, carpentry, weaving, braiding, stringing small beads, cutting, paper dolls, puzzles, target games, and yo-yos.

# SEVEN YEARS

## Physical

- Displays sudden spurts of active behavior in some task.
- Gets up frequently when sitting, becomes rather talkative.
- Interested in developing various motor skills.
- Will concentrate on one activity at a time, then lose interest.

## Emotional/Social

- Is concerned that school may be too difficult.
- Lacks confidence.
- Will approach new tasks or social situations with caution.
- Is concerned about how others perceive her.
- Is anxious for approval and acceptance by peers and adults.
- Interests in peer group and in belonging; enjoys special friends, cliques, gangs, secret languages, and passwords.
- Is more serious and thoughtful about life.
- Shows increased awareness of relationships with people around him.
- Shows interest in the community, immediate neighborhood, familiar experiences, and outside the immediate community.
- Is easily confused about responsibilities but eager to accomplish them.

- Shows interest in fair play and living up to standards (own and group's).
- Does not like to lose in games and may become very upset or cheat to win.

## Mental

### Writing/Language Arts:
- Strives for perfection.
- Uses the eraser a great deal.
- May still need widely spaced paper.
- Worries if written work is not done.
- Begins to control size and uniformity of letters.
- May find writing easier than printing.
- Enjoys copying words.
- Interested in and beginning to grasp the sounds of letters.
- Enjoys using pencils; tends to grasp pencils so tightly frequently drops them.
- Is undergoing further visual development.

### Reading:
- Reads mechanically.
- Omits or adds familiar or simple words.
- Omits or adds a final *s* or *y*.
- Can interpret story without knowing all of the words.
- Substitutes vowels.
- Hesitates or guesses at new words.
- Needs to know some follow-up activities after reading to build upon what is read.
- Interested in number of pages in a book.
- Show individual differences in reading speed.
- Beginning to be critical of reading materials.
- Enjoys fairy tales.

### Arithmetic:

- Male prefers oral and written activities.
- Female prefers concrete examples.
- Frequently reverses 2, 6, 7, and 9.
- Delights in writing long numbers.
- Easily confused if addition and subtraction problems appear on same page.

## Play

- Prefers playing with same-gender peers; increasing ability to play cooperatively.
- Enjoys climbing, but has a new awareness of height that makes for caution.
- Likes to alternate outdoor play between extremely active and sedate activities.
- Prefers realism to imaginative play.
- Is not well organized in group activity.
- May still prefer solitary play.
- Begins to discriminate against opposite sex.
- Finds pleasure in manipulating objects, creating with hands, and building complicated structures.
- Can play fairly well with four or five friends.
- Likes to produce finished products (art, models, crafts, sewing, carpentry).
- Interest in fantasy and reality—magic and tricks.
- Interested in other times and other places (history).
- Enjoys dramatic play (puppets, dolls, paper dolls, dress-ups).
- Enjoys attack-and-defense themes: police, cowboy, military, space.
- Interested in shows, plays, puppets.

# EIGHT YEARS

## Physical

- Has improved rhythm and grace in body movement.
- Shows increase in speed and smoothness of hand/eye performance.
- May develop nearsightedness.
- May display a gap between what she wants to do with her hands and what she can do.
- Improving in handwriting and printing.
- Likes to do neat work but frequently is in too great a hurry.
- Is accident-prone (generally in connection with falls and bicycles).

## Emotional/Social

- May react to disagreeable tasks or difficult school subjects with headaches, stomachaches, or frequent need to urinate.
- Shift from one interest to another.
- Spends much energy anticipating events.
- Tends to be argumentative and dramatic.
- Emotional when fatigued.
- Disappointed when feelings are hurt, if criticized, or if makes a mistake.
- Cries over dramatic stories or events.
- Displays fewer fears.
- Tends to be apprehensive about some activities if not confident or familiar.
- Worries about mistakes, failing, meeting standards.
- Will apply self even if subject is too difficult.
- Is quick to criticize.
- Exuberant in behavior.
- Will interrupt work to socialize with peers.

## Mental

- Enjoys school.
- Is eager to attack new tasks.
- Likes to talk.
- Impatient for directions to be given but tends to forget them.

### Writing/Language Arts:
- Shows individual differences in size and style of writing.
- Begins to space words and sentences.
- Has more ideas for a story than can write.

### Reading:
- Tackles new words by context or phonics.
- Tends to omit unimportant words.
- Reverses words in a phrase.
- Can stop and talk about the story without losing thread.
- Begins to prefer silent reading.
- Likes stories with excitement and humor.

### Arithmetic:
- Prefers oral to written.
- Likes to shift from one math process to another.

## At Play

- Has growing interest in games requiring small-muscle coordination.
- Enjoys group activities.
- Displays feelings of belonging.
- Generally more cooperative, but requires supervision to prevent dissension.
- Is interested in competitive games.
- Is becoming selective in choice of friends.
- Is seeking a "best friend" of same sex.

## SIX

# Older Child

## NINE TO TWELVE YEARS

Dave and Elaine merged three kids from previous marriages and were actively coping with a dynamic stepfamily and busy schedule. Elaine's two children, Matt, five, and Doug, eight, had many toys. They played enthusiastically, cooperatively, usually, and continuously.

Dave's daughter, Kari, eleven, who had no siblings, visited with them on weekends. She was, at first, more interested in being with her friends and made no attempt to relate to her younger brothers. Their toys and games were of no interest to her.

Dave and Elaine asked me what I could suggest to bring the whole family together. My goal was to propose activities that would have something appealing to five-, eight-, eleven-year-olds, *and* mom and dad.

Games like Monopoly, Parcheesi, and Scrabble have an amazingly broad base of interest for participants of different ages. Model-building and some crafts can incorporate different ability

**157**

levels and are another possibility. Perhaps the best is the "Family Read" as described on pages 123–24.

Kari had never had these intimate joint experiences before and though she was tentative at first, it wasn't long before she was caught up in sharing play with the rest of her stepfamily. She found it was more fun to have brothers than she expected. Smart Play, even for sophisticated eleven-year-olds, can widen important horizons.

## Changing, Changing, Ever Changing . . .

Children, as they enter puberty, are constantly transforming, in pace of growth, in attitudes, in moods. Sometimes the changes are very rapid; other times they are less noticeable. From the ages of nine through twelve, physical growth slows down for many children, especially for boys (girls of the same age are often taller than the boys), and they seem to reach a plateau. Some parts of their bodies may be out of proportion and, as a result, feelings of awkwardness and the appearance of poor coordination may be observed. For many children, this is the era of gangliness.

Adults often respond to the outward persona the child projects rather than to his true character. If a child is large, active, and well-coordinated, adults may react as if the child were older and very capable. If a youngster is awkward and ungainly, some adults assume this is integral to her nature and overlook clues to superior intelligence or talent.

If children from nine through twelve are not massively involved with school projects, either academic or extracurricular (like sports), they will derive greater benefits from a variety of games, arts, crafts, and hobbies, instead of trance-producing television. Even at this age range, they enjoy playthings, especially the challenging ones. Activities from earlier childhood will continue to entertain and teach on greater levels of sophistication.

## Peers of the Realm

Older children are centered on peer relationships more than ever before and show increased sensitivity, responsibility, and caring for friends.

There is a tendency for girls to mature more noticeably in verbal and creative ability in these years, while boys seem disposed to excel in math, scientific and technical aptitude, and construction, although such differences are by no means the rule. Boys like to play roughly in sports; girls gather in groups for jump-rope competition and other more quiet games. Preference for homogeneity prevails now, boys gather with boys, girls with girls. In mixed play both sexes give one another both positive and negative feedback about behavior. Teasing is becoming very big and sometimes hard to take. Play Tutor works hard on this and provides tips for handling such situations (deflecting/change of subject, humor, toppers if your child has a gift for this—but never overt displays of anger or exchanges of name-calling; that's the rise out of your son the bully is seeking). A most effective toy you might use for your Play Tutor lesson on handling teasing is a puppet/marionette for role-playing, or the use of any two figures, even stuffed animals, where your child plays her tormenter and you play her. You and your child then try out alternative responses.

After getting home from school, your child, whether boy or girl, needs time to relax and then, of course, do previously delineated chores. He also needs time to read, so keep appropriate books and magazines on hand.

## "I don't have any homework. . . ."

If you hear this response too often when you check with your daughter about schoolwork, you must intervene. Get her to tell you what she is studying. Talk with her about her textbooks and prepare assignments from them. Many have end-of-chapter review questions. Have her copy these out, or a selection of them, with their answers.

And, of course, get in touch with her teacher for a conference immediately; discover what his homework policy is, and deal with it accordingly.

Your youngster must do whatever homework is required. The third or fourth grader should be well into a homework habit by now—at least thirty minutes' worth each day. By high school this will mesh easily into the two to three hours a day appropriate for A and B grades.

Some children will need little prodding because they enjoy the work, while others need strong, supportive supervision, even direct involvement. However, *never* do homework for your child; coach, tutor, work with him, but don't supply answers, elicit them. Don't give answers to text questions, ask your own, and in a way that *she* figures out the correct facts.

By nine years old, your child must also have time to handle personal matters (hair, grooming, room cleanup, letters) and some time for phone calls. Do not allow these to get out of hand. If unrestrained, literally hours can be spent on conversation with a best buddy, especially among adolescent girls. Set up telephone ground rules now. When she's a teen, you'll be glad.

## About Video . . .

Peer influence may, unfortunately, lead a child to watch a lot of television. If you restrict TV viewing to an hour per day, his health—physical, emotional, and mental—will be vastly improved. The ideal is no more than two or three hours of TV *total* a week, and then for preselected programs—no channel surfing.

Your youngster should be firmly encouraged to explore activities other than incessant TV watching. Studies show that more children in the prepubescent and pubescent phases are in worse physical shape in the '90s than ever before. Establish time lines that allow a good balance for being with friends, for indoor play with toys and games, and for active and healthy outdoor activities for fitness. The whole family can enjoy walks, hikes, bike riding, and other sports. This is a good way for everyone to get in shape and stay that way.

## The Computer Age

Computers are entering classrooms in ever-increasing numbers and at earlier grades. During ages nine through twelve, home reinforcement, if possible, will keep your offspring abreast of the real world. By now, acquiring the skill of keyboarding is a must and if her school does not teach it, check with community enrichment programs (i.e., the YMCA) and enroll her.

## DR. TOY'S TIPS FOR SELECTING SOFTWARE FOR CHILDREN

1. Needs to be easy to understand.
2. Allows for exploration so it can be used independently.
3. Allows for a broad range of skills and concepts.
4. Gives a positive response for correct answers.
5. Corrects errors and explains them.
6. Provides valuable information.
7. Responsive and provides prompt feedback.
8. Includes good graphics, sound, animation, and is not violent
9. Appropriate for the child's developmental needs.
10. Is fun and enjoyable for the child.

## Hard Play, Quiet Play

Through active play, children learn the skills they need in school. Their muscles strengthen and sensory perceptions develop. Even during passive recreation like reading, children improve eye-muscle coordination, focus and concentrate for longer periods, perform visual and auditory discrimination, and become able to shift attention smoothly from parts to the whole and back again.

# NINE YEARS OLD

When the child is nine, you will observe that she is doing things with tremendous concentration and involvement, sometimes over-extending her abilities. She becomes more competitive in sports, in adventures with peers, and even in playing outdoors (skating, jump rope, tag, Hula Hoop). The nine-year-old is usually well-coordinated and has fine-motor control.

Making things, creating with craft, models, construction sets, role-playing with dolls or knights of the Round Table, dramatic play, experimenting with and using a broader spectrum of sports equipment, board games, and outdoor play make up your nine-year-old's world. They want to use their hands and explore their skills if given the opportunity. There are a great many model kits and craft sets available that will provide lots of opportunity for growing skills.

## The Declaration of Independence

This is a new age of autonomy. Your nine-year-old is exploring self-sufficiency and he will not like to be asked what he is up to. On the other hand, your boy or girl will cooperate with you if it is clear that you are reasonable. When she's out of the house, you *must* know where she is. Teach her to "check back" when she changes locations (by phone if at her friend's, in person if not). Not only is knowing where your child is at all times essential parenting, but if taught early (when he first goes into the neighborhood on his own) the habit will be established with a willing child and, as is usually the case, be so ingrained that it will continue through the teens—when it is needed more than ever! Your child wants to know that she is always important and that you also trust her to gain independence and build friendships and interests.

## Groups Are Good

A nine-year-old usually gets along well with his friends and groups. He likes being part of Cub Scouts, an athletic league, or a sports team. He and his friends may create clubs with secret passwords and meetings known only to members. A clubhouse, treehouse, or place they can play and talk is important.

But a nine-year-old can also be apprehensive, worrying about being accepted, her popularity with peers. She is learning how to work things out, and can fear failing. Parents must be sensitive to their child's changing moods and respect the ups and downs typical of preadolescents.

## The Little Rebel

The nine-year-old child may begin to show a natural rebellion and resist you (although at what age this gets under way varies greatly according to the personality of your child, even within the same family). You'll be challenged now, and the key to dealing effectively with negative behavior is to be consistent, fair-minded, patient, and firm. Be aware of "negative reinforcement": i.e., when negative behavior succeeds, it is reinforced. Don't let your child's nagging, belligerence, even attempts at intimidation, succeed in getting him something, or doing something, you know is not right for him. Hold the line. Just say "no"!

And never, *never* undercut your spouse in front of your child, or the child will learn to divide and conquer. Have a simple ground rule about this to which you and your spouse both consent. If you don't agree with the way your spouse is handling an incident, say nothing at the time. Speak privately as soon as is practicable. If you persuade your mate to your way of thinking, let *him* be the one to rearrange things, not you. If you cannot persuade him on this occasion, defer. Only if there is danger of serious harm to the child should you intervene in front of the child. A family council is another way for everyone to talk about any issues and reach resolution and compromise.

# TEN YEARS OLD

This child may sometimes be awkward and clumsy, but she tries hard and wants to get along. A definite difference appears in language use between boys and girls. Girls are often more advanced verbally and more socially poised. Boys tend to be more hesitant around girls, around strangers, and in new situations. Avoid words like "shy" when talking about your child, and not just within his hearing, as these terms only serve as negative labels and are demeaning.

## The Sporting Life!

The ten-year-old is active and sports are important. Girls may become proficient at jump rope, skating, and other activities they can do with a friend. Many boys are drawn to touch football and soccer. They are easily engrossed by TV (as most of it is on their mental level) and this is something you can offset with more active pursuits that encourage expression of energy.

When quiet time is appropriate, offer an irresistible book or an audiotape; remind your child of her model or craft project if necessary. Your child should learn to complete the task she decided to undertake and find satisfaction in the completed project. Give positive reinforcement when the project is finished. The more she finds satisfaction in doing things the more she will try to do these projects. She is learning to follow directions, figure things out, and finally see a task through from a plan to the final item. This is gratifying and can be a fun way to add decorations to her room. A model plane can be suspended from the ceiling on a hook and looks great. Other kids appreciate and talk about these projects among themselves.

# ELEVEN YEARS OLD

The group continues to be a prime social experience for the eleven-year-old, and the youngster becomes a fledgling, leaving the nest and meeting the world on his own terms. These older children assert their independence ever more strongly: doing things with friends without parental supervision; earning money to spend how they choose.

Create special jobs for your child around the house for which he can be paid. Many parents believe that basic allowances should be paid whether or not there are chores to complete; others feel their child must be made aware that a family works for and with one another, each contributing what he can to accomplish this. It all depends on the values most important in your family as to which approach you prefer: Your child's sense of being loved and accepted, regardless of what he can contribute, or his sense of being loved and accepted, and also respected for whatever he can offer. It is true for any child at any economic level that there is a sense of pride and self-worth that comes when your child feels he is relied upon and that what he does is important to everyone.

Nonroutine chores for extra money helps her to absorb the concept that there is "no free lunch" in the real world, and that the competence to earn and to be responsible for her expenditures is what it means to be adult—and to be a survivor. This most often has enormous appeal, as being "grown up" has real meaning at this age. Children need to learn to save money at this age. Help them open a bank account and encourage them to save money they earn or which was given as gifts.

The age in general is typically active, talkative, and playful. Most eleven-year-olds are eager learners and tend to copy one another. Time to pursue their own interests independently from the group becomes appealing, so classes in music, dance, or art are welcomed.

Typical eleven-year-olds focus on a few special friends and on getting involved with them in complicated projects like building a treehouse, working jointly on a science scheme, being a club member, making a dollhouse, riding bikes, fashioning things, and playing games together. They like listening to music and will read eagerly if they have been encouraged to do so all along.

# TWELVE YEARS OLD

By twelve, maturation of the child becomes clearly visible. There is a shift away from doing things because of peer pressure and toward intense feelings of hero worship, an idealization of one other person (older: brother, dad, uncle, teacher, celebrity figures like Tom Cruise or Julia Roberts, in whom they imbue fantasy qualities), whose style and habits the child will imitate. If the model is a good one, the child's behavior will show improvement and he will stay on course.

If this is not the case there may be a need to intervene with some counseling (your own to your child, of course, or from an intelligent and valued adult friend, or, if necessary, a professional). Keep goals simple, easy: turn her focus back to school, on activities you know she likes, and on positive friendships.

## Once a Parent, Always a Parent; Once a Child Is Enough!

As children grow, parental challenges do not diminish. When an adult child is on the brink of a bad decision, a parent still feels the need to caution him, he may protest but will generally accede to her right to give advice—as she should accede to his right to make the final decision.

Do not nag your child to do things that he is suddenly not interested in. Find out what is going on; try to be supportive. Your relationship is still the most important thing he has going for him, and down deep he knows it.

With allowances made for the inner-directed or the outer-directed child, your twelve- year-old's play will be predominantly experiences that involve varied competitive sports, both solo or on a team; acting with more independence; and creating things and following up on crafts and hobbies where she feels she has some ability and success. She'll continue to read, perhaps even voraciously, and she'll listen to the music for which she has acquired a taste.

You as a parent will always continue to be a vital factor in your youngster's happiness and well-being, and when he is twelve you will be confronted by decisions about his friends and personal styles. Try to accept, if not approve, differences in tastes (which are not yet fully matured) even if they are a drastic departure from yours. Some of the shifts the child is leaning toward are still within your ability to guide if you handle your input to him very carefully.

## The Mouth . . .

Your child will tend to be more emotional at this age (rampant hormonal changes go on now as well as many physical and mental adjustments). This can be a difficult period in your relationship and she may have discovered that bane of most parents—the sassy mouth.

It helps you if you will first acknowledge to yourself that:

1. This is a phase when assertion of self as an entity separate from you is taking place.
2. He *does* love and trust you. In fact, his awful behavior proves it. People like Oscar Wilde and the Mills Brothers memorialized the truism: "You always hurt the one you love. . . ."

Your child trusts that you'll love him still, even when he discharges emotions of frustration, tenseness, anxiety, and affirmation of his power, all of which are spurred into motion by his galloping hormones.

Two parents who support and respect each other is the best model for dealing with these behaviors. Keep calm, courteous, quiet, and firmly object to defiance and/or disrespect. Devise fair consequences—you might even ask what your youngster thinks is appropriate for what she did; this helps her "walk in other shoes" and view her own behavior objectively. Only in rare cases will a child not respond to this. Family counseling can offer help to reestablish improved communications when all else fails.

Adolescence is notorious for, in many families, a breakdown in relationships between parent and child. That's why teachers may seem far more effective with your child than you seem to be, and why some teachers establish excellent rapport and get cooperation from their students but feel they have no effect on their own offspring.

Keep in contact with your child by creating times when you can share informal play, crafts, or hobbies. Hang in there. You are ensuring that your child will be happy, positive, and a player in his or her everyday life.

Responsible twelve-year-olds may begin to baby-sit, caring for small children to earn extra money. Your sixth or seventh grader will happily use toys with the small children she tends, especially if you have shown her ways to use those toys effectively. You may want to refer your preteen to the earlier sections of this book as she begins sitting so she can become more familiar with some of the basics about baby, toddler, and preschooler.

This practice is sound training for his role as a parent later on. While he instructs young children in play and toys, he will reflect upon the kinds of experiences he had with you, as his memorable first Big Toy. This may well be an "aha!" time—the epiphany so many of us have had of suddenly being able to identify with mom or dad's viewpoint.

## TOY SUGGESTIONS FOR NINE- TO TWELVE-YEAR-OLDS

| | |
|---|---|
| 1. Arts and crafts/hobbies | (C) |
| 2. Board games | (E) |
| 3. Books | (C) |
| 4. Dolls | (E) |
| 5. Electronic games | (E) |
| 6. Miniatures | (C) |
| 7. Musical instruments | (C) |
| 8. Puzzles | (C) |
| 9. Scientific materials | (E) |
| 10. Transportation toys | (E) |

## SOME PRODUCTS AND ACTIVITIES FOR NINE THROUGH TWELVE

### 1. Arts and Crafts/Hobbies

Being creative is great for relaxation and for strengthening individual talents. Concentration and analytical skills have advanced so that quite complex projects can be achieved by your nine- to twelve-year-old: sewing garments, embroidery and samplers, knitting and crocheting, delicate model assembly, tool work on leather. The list abounds. Don't limit tasks by sex, either. Allow your son to knit or to make a leather jacket if this is what he wants to do.

A handmade product he will hang in his room, or give to a friend, parent, or grandparent, hones talents and provides enormous satisfaction of achievement. It doesn't matter what the specific art or craft is, as long as your child is enthusiastic about it. Other examples of crafts possible at this age are: weaving, quilting, dollmaking, collage, clay modeling, and pottery throwing.

Kits are available with instructions that will give your youngster a sample of wide possibilities. As a teacher, I found weaker readers could improve when I gave them hobby kits which required them to read instructions in order to build model cars or planes. They became highly motivated to ferret out the meanings they needed; discipline became much less of a problem.

Crafts take practice to build skill, but the results can be beautiful and rewarding. Many of these are handmade "take up" projects: perfect to take along on vacations, to do on rainy days, or when your child agrees to sit quietly during an adult gathering, mimicking, briefly, the Victorian child who was to be "seen and not heard."

You can find good selections in crafts and art supplies from ALEX, Avalon, Balitono, Binney & Smith, Craft House, Creativity for Kids, Curiosity Kits, Hero Arts, Natural Science Industries, Ohio Art, Pamela Drake Designs, Uncle Milton Industries, and Woodkrafter. $5–$35.

## 2. Board Games

When the power goes out, go back to basics! Why not pull the plug yourself? Bring out Monopoly, Parcheesi, Scrabble, checkers, or chess. Do you remember when you were a kid, eating popcorn and playing board games with your parents? Games continue to be a way families can have fun together, at home, on picnics and outings, during travel and vacations.

Buy games that fit your child's interest and your pocketbook. They come in many flavors, and offer challenge, communication, concentration, and camaraderie. Here are some favorites:

| | | |
|---|---|---|
| *Careers* | *Dark Tower* | *Monopoly* |
| *Checkers* | *Empire Builder* | *Parcheesi* |
| *Chess* | *Hail to the Chief* | *Risk* |
| *Civilization* | *Life* | *Scrabble* |
| *Clue* | *Master Mind* | *Trivial Pursuit* |

Games are available from many companies, including Aristoplay, Avalon, Binary Arts, Buffalo Games, Family Games, Gamewright, Koplow, Mayfair Games, Milton Bradley, Parker Brothers, Pressman, University Games, and U.S. System Wizards of the Coast. $10–$30.

## 3. Books

In the years between nine and twelve, your child is probably reading fluently two to three grade levels ahead of her own—*if* you have been able to follow my recommendations from early childhood, and by now have a well-established Family Read, even if only a few times a week.

Reading is a far more constructive activity than watching TV; it stimulates the mind and the imagination so that the individual comes to *prefer* the horizons of his own speculations to passively watching TV scenarios.

One function of reading is to provide information for the child when there is a difficulty in her communicating with you on a subject. Children need information on sex and their bodies: biology, hygiene, hormonal changes, growth, and other natural functions or puzzling relationships.

Select books carefully. Be sure there is nothing that contradicts your own values. Verify that the reading level is at your youngster's—neither too simplistic nor too dry and difficult. Encourage her to ask you questions about things she does not understand in the book. Elicit her reactions, how she feels about what she's learning. Be sure your own attitude is mellow, accepting, encouraging, and allow her to check out her perplexing experiences with you.

Remember your own childhood. Wasn't it a long, intricate tapestry of sensations and feelings from your earliest recollections to preadolescence? There were new changes taking place in your body, and with the arrival of strange emotions, moods, and urges, there was much confusion at times.

Provide full information *and in an ethical context that underscores your own values!* Be sure to have explanations for your moral position that are reasonable, specifically relevant, and pragmatic, not "just because I say so," or "the Bible tells us so." In the late twentieth century most children can no longer be influenced in this manner.

Further, combining ethics with logic (and ethics *are* logical) provides the parameters that will help your offspring feel more secure; if he knows what is happening he can face these enigmas and deal with them. The librarian at your public library can assist you and your child to develop a recommended reading list of appropriate and interesting titles available through the library. If your child finds that a particular author is of great interest you can show him where to obtain these books at the nearest bookstore. Books make great gifts at all ages.

Books are published by Bobbs-Merrill; Delacourte; Doubleday; EDC; HarperCollins; Knopf; Little, Brown; McGraw-Hill; Penguin; Random House; and Simon & Schuster. $3–$10.

## 4. Dolls

Older children still play with dolls and eleven- and twelve-year-old girls especially like the adult-figured, fashion dress-up dolls. Collecting dolls can become an activity that lasts well into adulthood, and now is the time some youngsters begin to save up for the stunning porcelain and bisque figures, with delicately crafted, very individual faces, gowned in incredible creations from the nineteenth century. These dolls are costly ($200–$500) and are obtainable from the Franklin Mint and Ashley Drake collections among others.

Attractive, less expensive dolls have been designed to represent '90s values. It's encouraging to see role models for girls reflected in dolls dressed in historical styles, jogging clothes, or dancing tights and who look like they do an hour of aerobics every day. Girls will enjoy going to a doll show to see the great variety available among collectible dolls.

Boys also have collections, perhaps of action figures or replicas of heroic persons from the past and the present. Chess men in fantastic images attract the young chess player—*Star Trek*, sword and sorcery, meticulously crafted Civil War sets to name but a few.

Boys will find models and action figures from Galoob, Hasbro, Mattel, Reeves, Tyco, and others. $3–$25.

Dolls are made by Alexander Doll, Corolle, Effanbee, Goetz, Kathe Kruse, Mattel, Olmec, Pleasant Company, Vogue Dolls, and many others. $10–$35.

## 5. Electronic Games

Although electronic games can be intriguing, they can also be gimmicky, violent, and actually mind-damaging. Encourage your child to interact primarily with other children and less with a machine, whether electronic games, television, or the computer. Balanced activities are key during these years, because this is when your offspring is most vulnerable to obsessive fads.

Even if you do consider an electronic game, be sure that it is informative or will ready a young mind for a desirable skill (instead of cookies eating other cookies, which has absolutely no intrinsic value, you might search out a simulated vehicle-driving game).

The following list of games can assist you in making your choice. Examine each game carefully for its value to your child before buying. Shop around for the ones that offer the most learning potential, skills readiness, and flexibility. Don't be swayed by your child's ploys or by current advertising. Packaging and promotion can make anything look good.

SUGGESTED ELECTRONIC GAMES:

| | |
|---|---|
| Automobile Drive | Football |
| Backgammon | Golf |
| Baseball | Hockey |
| Basketball | Miniature Golf |
| Bridge | Skiing |
| Chess | Soccer |
| Fishing | Tennis |

## 6. Miniatures

The naturally collectible miniatures include figures, animals, doll-house furnishings, soldiers, vintage cars, race cars, small houses, and farm buildings—today, just about any environmental figure can be found as a miniature.

These minitoys are formed from molded plastic, cast metal, or carved wood, and can be very detailed. Many collectibles are action-oriented.

A word of caution. Miniatures absolutely must have well-planned storage: a special box just for a set, even a locked showcase. Under no circumstances should these toys be left around if a small child can come upon them. They become dangerous if put in the mouth.

Miniatures are made by dozens of manufacturers, including Britains, Ertl, Just Kids, Mattel, and Tyco. $5–$12.

## 7. Musical Instruments

By this age, if your child is interested in playing a musical instrument, you will soon see if she is sincere. If she practices for some time every day without needing to be reminded, or if after several months she still shows enthusiasm *and* you detect improvement, see that she has a well-qualified music teacher and the best instrument that teacher recommends—and which you can afford. Until then, rent the instrument. Don't invest in an expensive sax, trumpet, or violin right away. Your child's attention may be short-lived.

Some children are eager to play in a school band. Your child will continue in the band if his teacher is inspiring, he likes the experience, and he has the talent. And your youngster may well turn out to be quite musically gifted.

Playing music at home gives him opportunities to offer his muse to a greater audience, but let it be natural and comfortable. Don't force him to perform.

Musical instruments are made by Douglas, Hohner, Magnus Organ Company, Reeves International, and Yamaha. $10–$55.

## 8. Puzzles

Now the child will choose quite complicated puzzles with many more pieces. Your youngster will enjoy them more if she can do the puzzle when she wants to. Lay it out on some flat surface where it will not be disturbed and let her return to the project as she can find time.

Puzzles are made by American Publishing Company, DaMert, Frank Schaffer, Milton Bradley, and Wrebbit. $5–$15.

## 9. Scientific Materials

If your offspring shows an interest in chemistry or some other aspect of science, encourage him. Find materials that supplement what he learns in school, like chemistry sets, and kits for biology, physics, astronomy, and geology experiments to name but a few. You can find science projects in special stores and in catalogs. Talk to your child's science teacher if you want to find more.

Science materials are available from Capsella, Educational Insights, Insect Lore, Natural Science Industries, Scientific Explorer, Tasco, and Uncle Milton Industries. $5–$25.

## 10. Transportation Toys

These attract and will retain the child's interest for a long time. At ages nine and up, she will be fascinated by remote-controlled cars, boats, or train sets. Creating realistic scenes and dioramas for train sets is part of the allure.

If your youngster is interested in transportation, get him a cap which identifies him as Motorperson, Engineer, big semitrucker, and of course, purchase the vehicles he wants. He will act out the Indy 500, or backing his train to take on cattle. Your daughter may play at transporting her horse to the Kentucky Derby.

Transportation toys include many types. Depending on your child's interests a train set may be the best investment or he may prefer model cars, especially battery-operated or radio-control models. Transportation products are available from Bachmann, Bandai, Hasbro, LGB, Lionel, Marlon Creations, Mattel, Nikko, and OWI. $3–$150.

| | | |
|---|---|---|
| Airplanes | Model kits | Transformers |
| Boats | Motorcycles | Trucks |
| Cars | Service station | |
| Farm equipment | Trains | |

Older children have a wide range of interests. They continue to enjoy play, but are able to handle more complexity—in games, projects, products, and activities. The following checklist will help you match your child's interest to possible products. You will learn a lot if you listen to what your child likes and why. You may not agree of course, but understand his preferences as a sign of his own personality growth and emerging peer relationships that are exceedingly important at this age.

## CHECKLIST OF SUGGESTED TOYS AND PRODUCTS FOR CHILDREN NINE TO TWELVE

| | | | |
|---|---|---|---|
| Arts | Chemistry sets | Kites | Stuffed animals |
| Baton | Computer | Oil-painting | Tape recorder |
| Binoculars | Construction | Papermaker | Tapes |
| Books | sets | Pets | Telescope |
| Camera | Crafts | Sewing machine | Typewriter |
| Camping | Exercise tapes | Software | Workbench and |
| equipment | Flower press | Sports | tools |
| CDs | Juggling sets | equipment | Yo-yo |

## ▶ DEVELOPMENTAL MILESTONES OF OLDER CHILDREN

# NINE YEARS

## Physical
- Works and plays hard; is apt to overdo.
- Displays increased skill and interest in motor performance and competitive sports.

## Emotional/Social
- Acts in the spirit of service.
- Capable of planning daily activities.
- Persists in completing what has been planned.
- Easily absorbed in what he is doing.
- Initial stages of hero worship.
- Is beginning to develop real feelings of empathy.
- Tends to be impressed with whatever she is told.

## Mental
- Enjoys school.
- Interested in achieving.
- Is easily discouraged by failure.
- Interested in discovering how errors made.
- Displays a spontaneous interest in problem-solving.
- Individual differences are apparent in change from third to fourth grade.
- Child who earlier had difficulties in learning may now show a spurt in improvement; child who had previously done well may now require special assistance in some areas.

**Reading:**

* Prefers silent reading.
* Likes to read for fact and information.
* Displays independence, self-discipline, an ability to evaluate herself and her skills.
* Displays difficulties in immediate recall.

## At Play

* Hand/eye coordination and fine-motor skills are well advanced.
* Child eager to have a good relationship with those around him.
* Has special friends selected from her own sex.
* Enjoys verbalizing with peers.
* Shows more organization in play than earlier.
* Organizes informal clubs which have a real purpose for short periods of time; generally likes codes, secret language, bulletins.
* Wants to be part of organizations like Brownies or Cub Scouts.

**Prefers:**

* Construction materials (varied materials for detailed construction and for creating models: tiny nuts, bolts).
* Puzzles.
* Creating permanent designs (art and craft materials).
* Bead-stringing, braiding, weaving, spool-knitting, and sewing.

# TEN TO TWELVE YEARS

## Physical

* Dramatic rate of growth.
* Inclined to be clumsy if in a growth spurt.
* Unaware of space needed to operate in, i.e., reaching- and stepping-distance differences.
* Aware of body changes and the onset of puberty.
* Prefers to undress in isolation: self-conscious about changing body.

- Will want to shower or bathe either frequently or never.
- Likes jeans and sneakers, the shabbier the better!
- Has firm food preferences; those preferences, as with other ages, depend upon exposure to a variety of foods, experience with home and regular diet, and peer pressure.
- Puppy love and sexual exploration may take place; boys may experience wet dreams.
- A time of extremes in behavior related to health habits.

## Emotional/Social

- A time of great peer pressure for group conformity.
- May display need to be independent and "grown up."
- May need more support than ever in changing social world.
- Notices opposite sex.

## Mental

- Child is preparing for junior high or high school; may be somewhat apprehensive.
- A critical time for parent/Play Tutor to be an active, nonjudgmental listener; parents able to meet this need will find that it is easier to develop a rich relationship throughout adolescence.

## At Play

- Period in which sports may play a significant role.
- Street sports and organized sports seem to attract.
- Construction or workbench materials to make models are appealing.
- Earlier childhood play activities will continue to be enjoyed because of improved skills.

# CHECKLIST OF PLAY MATERIALS

This list summarizes many products in the chapter and provides additional suggestions:

- Printing materials, typewriters, materials for making books.
- Math manipulatives, fraction and geometrical materials.
- Measuring materials—balance scales, rulers, graded cups for liquids, etc.
- Science materials—prism, magnifying materials, stethoscope.
- Natural materials to examine and classify.
- Plants and animals to study and care for.
- Computer programs for language arts, numbers, geography, history, science, and concept development, and for problem-solving activities.
- Simple card and board games, word games, reading and spelling games, guessing games.
- Memory games, number and counting games (like dominoes and Parcheesi).
- Beginning strategy games (checkers, chess, Chinese checkers).
- Books at a different levels of difficulty, storybooks, poetry, rhymes, humorous books, adventure books, myths, books made by children.
- Arts-and-craft materials (a variety of crayons, markers, colored pencils, art chalks, pastels, paintbrushes, paints, watercolors; variety of art papers for drawing, tracing, painting; scissors; pastes and glues [nontoxic]); collage materials.
- Clay tools (including pottery wheel).
- Craft materials, looms, leather, papier-mâché, plaster of Paris, small beads for jewelry making, workbench with tools and wood for projects..
- Musical instruments: recorders, drums, bells, and other instruments.
- Tapes, music for movement, including dancing (folk dancing).

- Music, singing, rhymes, and stories for listening.
- Audiovisual materials that children can use independently.
- Ride-on equipment.
- Small figures for play and fantasy scenes.
- Materials (to make props and costumes) for plays and performances.
- Materials for constructing play scenes and models.
- Construction materials.
- Puzzles (three-dimensional, fifty- to one-hundred-piece jigsaws, map puzzles).
- Projects teaching skills like printing, bookmaking, math, measuring, handling money, telling time.
- Science materials (weather, solar system, plant/animal life, basic human anatomy).
- Pattern-making materials (mosaic tiles, geometric puzzles).
- Games to develop interaction skills, planning, using strategies, understanding rules; reading, spelling, math games; guessing games; memory games; card games.
- Recorded music for group singing, moving, and rhythm activities and equipment for listening and recording.
- Variety of balls and equipment for specific sports (kickball, simple target games).
- Outdoor and gym equipment (climbing gym, swings, slides, ladders, seesaw).
- Mirrors and prisms.
- Dolls, washable for everyday play, rubber/vinyl baby dolls (culturally relevant features and skin tones); accessories; caretaking items: feeding, diapering, sleeping.
- Creating and practicing real-life activities—play money, calculator, cash register, checkbook.
- Puppets of familiar and fantasy figures for acting out stories.
- Simple puppet theater child can create with props and scenery.
- Stuffed toys/play animals, realistic rubber, wood, or vinyl animals for scenes.

- Small people/animal figures and materials to construct fantasy scenes or models.
- Transportation toys including small, exact replicas.

## WHY NOT COMMUNITY PLAY CENTERS?

Children always need safe places to play. I would like to see every community create Community Play Centers to develop learning, physical activity, and creativity in or near the schools. The facilities would include a host of activities, including computer and board games that teach children needed skills and strategy. Other activities would include arts, crafts, music, theater, dance, and reading.

- The center would schedule usage times by age or aptitude groups, during which youngsters with similar abilities could share activities. In turn children would have supervised play outdoors. See pages 228–30 for more details.

# SEVEN

# Special Needs

Children with special needs run the gamut from a severely disabled youngster to a child who is intellectually gifted far beyond the norm. For children with disabilities, properly selected playthings allow learning with less pressure to achieve and without generating a fear of failure. Because some play tasks are more challenging for a disabled child, he may not be motivated to play alone with the toy or game. Some handicapped children lack sufficient attention span to focus for more than a few minutes.

Play with your child on her level. Don't impose rigid rules, or both child and parent may quickly become frustrated. Observing and following the child's cues is basic to discovering what is appropriate to give her.

For example, one parent lamented: "I don't enjoy reading to my child. He doesn't like it either. He keeps stopping me to tell what he sees in the pictures. He wants to tell the story himself." But as I told the parent, this is wonderful! His child is demonstrating two things: a marvelous creativity and a short attention span. The latter is unimportant. Let it improve at the child's own pace.

Focus on her creativity and encourage it. It helps exercise her mental muscles.

Depending on the type and degree of the child's handicap, toys for a child's chronological age may or may not be suitable. The reaction of a young disabled child to a new toy could be upbeat and rewarding or negative and discouraging. Gear your selections accordingly.

A challenged child will typically react with overt responsiveness to a toy he likes, but will be silent about a toy not meaningful to him. This youngster should have a good variety of safe toys, including some which offer a moderate degree of challenge. Your pediatrician, social worker, or therapist, nearest Lekotek Center, and special organizations focused on special needs are resources for specific help. Look at the resources section (pages 192–95) for more organizations that can be of assistance.

Questions to ponder when selecting toys for the disabled are the same as those for any other child, but for the exceptional child, keep in mind her specific skills, needs, abilities, and readiness. Consider these elements:

• Physical strength, coordination and physical readiness. Observe your child moving, reaching, crawling, and pulling. Which needs more help? What can you provide to strengthen his muscles? Can you attract the child's attention? Can he see details on the toy? Can he visually follow objects like your moving finger? Does she respond to sounds? To action? To touch? Where is the child's focus? How can you assist in helping her with: reaching out and holding on to an object, letting it go, fitting things together, stringing beads? Can you show her how to snap and unsnap, turn over, pull things apart, fit pieces together, fit shapes into forms, dump out and put back, compare big and little? Is he able to handle cutting, drawing a picture, writing, throwing, catching, climbing? Have you tried helping him work with clay, finger paint, and dressing himself?

- Mental ability and emotional developmental levels. How can you assist your child to notice differences? See similarities? Does he notice letters? Words? Feel good about himself? Will he look at the mirror? Pat parts of body and identify eyes, nose, mouth, ears? Does she gain self-control? Understand directions? Read letters? Understand important street signs? Read important other signs? Is she aware of word meanings such as hot, cold, up, down, large, small? Will she be able to read? At what level?
- Attention span and concentration skills. Can you assist her in: holding the rattle, putting rings on a stack, taking something apart and putting it together? How can you help him see where something has been hidden, find something, fit pieces of a puzzle together? When can you expect him to respond to a story; tell what came first; see what is big and little, tall and short, red and blue?
- Ability to play with the toys alone or with others. How can you assist your child to feel good about what he accomplishes, feel pride in small tasks? Must you actually teach her how to play alone, get along with another child for a period of time, or share things?
- Potential enjoyment of the toy. Can you assist your child to enjoy a variety of toys? With your help, can she explore new things and learn from them? Make discoveries and be proud of them?
- Development. Children with special needs should be treated no differently than other developing children and with loving consideration of their disabilities. Parents' attitudes sometimes can get in the way of their child's progress toward growth and independence. Be as sensitive as you can to his feelings. Your *own* emotions are influential and must be handled positively. Identify your feelings. If you and/or your spouse have difficulty accepting any of your child's problems, take family counseling with a reputable therapist. These professionals have different styles, and it's OK to "shop" for the right one. Do not remain with anyone with whom you, your spouse, or your child is not comfortable.

## Language Development

When any of the senses are impaired, your special child can compensate by strengthening his other senses. When he experiences difficulties in areas like language, a speech therapist (in this instance) will teach him how to utilize substitute senses and muscle connections.

If your child has difficulty in being understood or not using sentences by the age of three or if she seems to be embarrassed about her speech or is nonfluent by the age of six, consult with your pediatrician and a speech pathologist. Your youngster will be tested to determine the nature of the problems, and you will be given a plan that will assist you in helping her.

If you converse with him and explain life around him, he can gain language faster. Everything you do at home is part of building communication skills, including tasks like washing dishes, preparing meals, eating, shopping, cleaning, washing the car, getting him dressed, giving him his bath, and helping him take care of a pet. Often trips and errands incorporate new vocabulary and language concepts into his permanent memory.

Smart Play goals are: helping your child express feelings, recognize sounds, attach meaning to words, recall the past, express her needs, describe what she sees and hears, and realize that others understand and appreciate her.

A child's feelings of anger, frustration, or upset come out when he plays. Let him try out behaviors that help him communicate, otherwise he will develop secondary emotional frustrations and problems.

WHAT YOU CAN DO TO EXPAND YOUR CHILD'S
COMMUNICATION SKILLS:

- Talk to her about traveling and concepts of coming and going, waiting, expecting mail or a package.
- Discuss going to the store, being at the store, and then take him so he can see what goes with your words.

- Describe and talk about the different toys she has and elicit her feelings about them.

Some children may have difficulty in speaking smoothly because they are excited, or their thoughts go more quickly than they can speak. Such nonfluency is sometimes called stuttering. If you do not make much of this condition it can work itself out. Reduce the amount of pressure that is on your child at any particular moment. When you jump in to complete a word for him, or otherwise draw attention to the halting speech, it usually makes matters worse.

## DR. TOY'S TIPS ON USING TOYS FOR SPECIAL NEEDS

- Talk with your child and encourage him to speak. Use playtime as a time to play—together.
- Use one toy at a time.
- Spend time on the floor with your child. It's a safe place to play and makes it easy for both of you.
- Use real words for things as much as you can. The more language you use the better.
- Take time each day for expressive activities like speaking short words and phrases, practicing short sentences, and reading aloud.
- Play at your child's level.
- Do not strain your child; stop when she shows signs of frustration or weariness.
- Teach the child how to behave with other children: taking turns, being fair, not hurting anyone.
- Encourage him to trade toys but not to pull them out of another's hands.
- Notice the characteristics of the toy which benefits your child the most, and look for them on new purchases.

The resources available for products that help children are diversified and there are many guides to those that you can make yourself. A few ideas for handmade items are:

- Feel-y Bag: a fabric bag where different objects are placed and the child guesses what they are without looking.
- Play clay: see recipe on page 97.
- Scrapbook: crop photos of child and family and create a book with covers that you make yourself.
- Toy bag: can be made from a pillowcase; it's the place where your child can keep preferred quiet-time toys.
- Domino cards: on unruled index cards (5X7) you can make matching numbers and circles on both sides; match the opposite sides of the cards so the child can identify the circles and numbers.
- Shape sorter: cut a circle, triangle, and square out of a lid to a container (each opening has to be larger than a quarter); your child will enjoy matching the shape and the cut-out piece.

## Play Learning

The exceptional child will often find some types of learning and skill development frustrating. Learning proceeds faster when there is excitement and pleasure. Toys, therefore, are particularly helpful in maintaining the interest of the disabled child while he acquires essential skills. For example, a barnyard playset offers many opportunities for developing a wide number of skills:

## VISUAL SKILLS

1. Color matching between objects.
2. Matching pairs of animals.
3. Discriminating between objects and animals.

## Concept Development
1. Color recognition and labeling.
2. Number concepts.
3. Associative concepts—animals and their young.

## Fine-Motor Skills
1. Manipulating doors, moving animals, vehicles.
2. Constructing fences.

## Auditory Skills
1. Matching animals to their sounds (emitted by the Play Tutor).
2. Making sounds of tractor and animals.

## Language Development
1. Recognizing animals, barnyard parts, equipment by name.
2. Naming things in the barnyard.
3. Learning rhymes and songs associated with farm, farmer, animals.
4. Describing actions taking place on farm.
5. Finding pictures of farms and cutting them out for scrapbook.

# PRODUCTS/ACTIVITIES THAT HELP BUILD SKILLS

The following toys and play activities are recommended for developing specific skill areas in young children with learning disabilities:

LANGUAGE
Cooking
Feel-y bag
Finger play
Miniatures
Playsets (dollhouses,
  farm, garage or
  circus)
Puppets
Rhymes
Stories

AUDITORY
Drums and
  tambourines
Finger play
Music
Sound cans
Storytelling
Talking toys

FINE MOTOR
Beads and string
Bristle blocks
Feel-y (tactile)
  toys
Finger paint
Lacing toys
LEGOs
Peg-Boards
Play dough
Play tools

VISUAL
Blocks
Matching objects
puzzles
Multi-colored toys
Peg-Boards
GROSS MOTOR
Beanbags
Jungle gym
Large blocks
Minitrampoline
Rocking horse
Scooter boards

CONCEPT DEVELOPMENT
Graduated
  cylinders and
  cubes
Real-life toys
Sequence games
Small objects to
  be counted

## Blind or Visually Impaired Children

Large-muscle play equipment is necessary to discharge tension normally released through running. Bouncers and swings for babies are perfect. Slides and gym bars for older children are helpful. Because of their tactile and kinesthetic value, finger paint, play dough, and paste are important creative-art materials for blind children.

Materials with varying textures and tactile attributes (texture-matching puzzles and texture-matching boards) are recommended. Sound-making and musical toys are beguiling to those who cannot see. A homemade collection of sound makers (metal measuring spoons, wooden spoons, rice-filled cans, etc.) is not only educational, but also noisily cheering.

## Hearing-Impaired Children

The encouragement of speech is a primary goal for hearing-impaired children, and so toys and games that develop language are recommended. For example, singing, sharing in nursery rhymes, and finger plays will help achieve emulation of sound. Your hearing therapist will demonstrate techniques on how to do this.

Materials which are self-correcting, such as those introduced by Montessori, are excellent because they allow the hearing-impaired child to monitor his own performance, master cognitive skills and concept formation, and develop a feeling of competence. Visual materials (puzzles, dominoes, and matching games) are also useful because they enforce the concepts of problem-solving and logical thinking which are transferable skills that will help the child deal with her hearing loss.

## Physically Handicapped

Because his movement may be restricted, equipment and toys that provide mobility are eagerly sought after by the physically limited youngster. A rocking horse, scooter board, tricycles, swing, wagon, or cart is recommended for children with motor disabilities. Playing ball with a beanbag or a soft cloth ball, Nerf, or Koosh ball is preferable. Since these children may have impaired abilities to use their hands, soft, flexible objects are best.

The size of manipulatives such as pegs, puzzle pieces, and blocks should also be taken into consideration and individualized for your child's needs. Sand or water play is especially desirable, giving needed exercise or soothing relaxation depending upon how the Play Tutor manages the activity.

## PRACTICAL RESOURCES FOR THE SPECIAL CHILD'S PLAY

As there are often poorer copies of products produced abroad and imported to the U.S., be sure that what you purchase is full value and has an established brand name.

### Lekotek: Toy Library for the Disabled

A network of toy libraries (Lekotek) offers special adaptations of toys for disabled children. Lekotek toy libraries exist throughout the country with well-trained staff to assist you in your child's play and learning needs. Toys are carefully adapted and are on loan with special instructions and training on how the child should play with them to his best advantage.

Appropriate toys are offered which emphasize play and development. You will be taught specific ways to use the special products with your child and how the playthings can provide stimulation of muscles and senses, and impart knowledge and skills.

Plan and ask questions. There are books and other materials to help you with decisions and selections. Lekotek's trained staff is ready to help you with any difficulty. Talk the situation over with your contact person on staff, and if he doesn't have an answer himself for you, he will know how to find out what you need to know.

For further information about a program nearest you contact:

National Lekotek Center
2100 Ridge Avenue
Evanston, IL 60201
(800-366-7529)

## Kanor Catalog

Dr. Steven Kanor has been a pioneer in the area of adaptive toys and other materials for many years. He is a sincere and committed professional who provides many additional resources through his extensive catalog. This fine catalog has been developed by Dr. Kanor in cooperation with the staff of the Toy Library. Dr. Kanor understands technology and illustrates the right way to assemble these special toys and enabling devices so they can be used by special-needs children.

Special switches are available for action toys, for example, to enable only a slight pressure, puff, or movement to make the toys move.

Other examples include:

- A device that speaks phrases when the child presses a square, symbol, or word.
- A dome filled with colors and lights.
- A clown that has eyes that light up and makes other sounds and melodies.
- Special motorized vehicles.
- Adapted Wimmer-Ferguson mobile with motor so the graphics can be seen from any angle and can be changed from time to time.

- Stuffed animals that bark, purr, and make other sounds; light up; and also make music.
- Busy boxes providing auditory stimulation, sounds, and lights.
- Music boxes.
- Baby dolls that light up.
- Devices, switches, computer keyboards, TV remote controller, and lights, plus many other products that help the disabled child.

Contact Toys for Special Children to obtain their forty-eight-page catalog of adapted toys:

Toys for Special Children
385 Warburton Avenue
Hastings on Hudson
New York, NY 10706
800-TEC-TOYS/914-478-0960

## Crestwood Aids

Another good resource is the catalog of Crestwood Company Communication Aids for Children and Adults. Their catalog lists a variety of educational materials, amplifiers, switches, card sets, sorting and counting kits, interactive toys, and more. Contact:

Crestwood Company
Communication Aids for Children and Adults
6625 North Sidney Place
Milwaukee, WI 53209
414-352-5678

## Seminars and Catalogs

The catalog of Dr. Lawrence E. Shapiro, Center for Applied Psychology, is a useful resource. Pertinent products for children who have specific psychological and emotional needs are listed. These include adjustment issues of aggression, impulsive behavior, upsets due to divorce, anger, and such specific disabilities as ADHD (Attention Deficit Hyperactivity Disorder). The catalog offers an array of books and games, and also enrichment devices. Listed as well are training materials and seminars for professionals and parents. Contact:

> Center for Applied Psychology
> P.O. Box 61586
> King of Prussia, PA 19406
> 800-962-1141

## Additional resources

> Exceptional Parent Magazine
> P.O. Box 3000 Dept. EP
> Denville, NJ 07834
> 800-247-8080

# THE SICK OR HOSPITALIZED CHILD

When a child is at home and sick, quiet activities can keep her amused. Consider books, crayons, coloring books, simple hobby kits, construction toys, games, paper dolls, audio or videocassettes, plush toys, and puppets.

If a child is in the hospital, talk with the Child Life Specialist or play-activities coordinator, who will assist in providing particular activities that will amuse, educate, and entertain him when he is recovering from treatment. The specialist will help him cope with his feelings, fears, and pains.

Role-playing is a successful way to give emotional support to a child who is ill, but well enough to be distracted. Use puppets, dolls, and stuffed animals to make his transition easier. They will be familiar figures in an otherwise strange environment.

Remain with your child as much as possible. The Ronald

McDonald House is located near many hospitals to provide for overnight parent stays. When you are with her be calm, patient, and positive. Your upbeat attitude will go a long way toward giving your child the optimism that helps her heal.

Select appropriate toys by ALEX, Anatex, Applause, Binney & Smith, Briarpatch, BRIO, Colorforms, Fisher-Price, Learning Curve, Learning Materials Workshop, LEGO SYSTEMS, Manhattan Toys, North American Bear Company, PlaySkool, and Today's Kids.

## THE GIFTED CHILD

Every child is, in his or her own way, gifted. She may be intellectually bright, musically or artistically talented, or blessed with a serene and happy view of life. The gifted child requires special attention from her parents as much as children who are intellectually challenged, or who have a physical disablement. Gifted children have needs which their parents must fulfill.

As do all children, the gifted child needs love but he also must have controls: attention, discipline, parental involvement, and training in self-reliance and independence. Emphasize early verbal expression and early reading.* Discuss adult ideas in his presence. Expose him to poetry and music.

Parents of the gifted child age six or above should consider finding him a playmate who is also gifted, even if the child has to be "imported" from some distance. Friendships with other children of the same age are most important, but especially to

---

*Reading readiness depends upon visual maturation. Young children tend to be farsighted, and this usually rights itself by age five or six, when the average child can then perceive the page in focus. Many children could begin reading as early as three years old if it were not for this. However, some children may eventually be myopic (nearsighted) and so when they are three and four they *can* focus on a page. Therefore, your child may be gifted and she may also be farsighted, so do take that into consideration and be very patient.

the gifted child who may, because of her superior mentality, become a loner.

Parents should show initiative in taking the gifted child to museums, art galleries, educational institutions, and historical sites where various collections may stimulate and enhance background learning.

Parents should be especially careful not to "shut up" the child who asks questions. Sometimes questions should not be answered *per se*; allow your reply to be a question which elicits the answer from his own thinking. If you don't know the answer, admit it. (She'll respect you for this.) Then take your child to a resource and show her how to research the answer for herself.

Though the gifted child usually has a wide and versatile range of interests, he may be less able to concentrate on one area for a long time, depending upon his age. Encourage your child to have "take up/put down" hobbies, crafts, and art activities to practice extending her follow-through.

Avoid direct, indirect, or unspoken attitudes of displeasure toward fantasy, originality, unusual questions, imaginary playmates, or out-of-the-ordinary mental processes on the part of your child. Do not allow him to feel they are bad, "different," or to be discouraged. Never laugh *at* a child, laugh *with* her, and seek to develop a sense of humor—your own as well as hers!

Don't overstructure your gifted's life. Give him free time for himself. Sometimes parents are concerned that gifted children should not spend any time watching TV or reading comic books. Your gifted cannot be expected to perform at top capacity at all times. TV can be interesting, relaxing, and educational if you introduce selected programs wisely.

Respect the child and her knowledge, which often may be better than your own. Do not presume on your authority as a parent except in crises. Allow liberty on unimportant issues. Give general instructions, and let him carry them out in his way, rather than giving specific commands to be carried out in yours. The enrichment potential of this policy is inestimable.

Whenever possible, talk things out with your gifted child, especially when there has been a disciplinary lapse. Gifted children are much more amenable to rational argument and at an earlier age than are many children, and will usually have a well-developed sense of duty.

Take time to be with your child, to listen to what she says, to discuss ideas. Be a good example yourself, and try to find worthwhile adults of both sexes outside the family for the child to know.

Support school efforts to plan for able children. Attend study groups on gifted children. With other parents, form cooperative activities and share resources.

# PLAY RESOURCES FOR EXCEPTIONAL CHILDREN

The following lists are additional play resources to consider using for assisting any child with special needs and to strengthen skills in specific areas as noted:

AUDITORY STIMULATION
- *blocks*
- *chime balls*
- *clocks*
- *mirror*
- *music boxes*
- *rattles*
- *shakers*
- *squeaking toys*
- *tambourines*

VISUAL AND AUDITORY
- *music boxes*
- *musical instruments*
- *rattles*
- *squeeze toys that make sounds*

FOCUS ON OBJECTS
- *balls*
- *bracelets*
- *flutter balls*
- *plastic keys*
- *rattles*
- *teething rings*
- *windup toys*

EXERCISE
- *balls*
- *cradle gyms*
- *suction toys that can take hits without falling over*

MOVING AND SHAKING
- *musical instruments*
- *rattles*
- *shakers: small things inside film cases with tops*
- *shapes*
- *symbols*

PUSHING/PULLING
- *bells*
- *busy boxes*
- *cluster balls*
- *cymbals*
- *musical instruments*
- *rattles*
- *spools*

EXAMINING OBJECTS
- *blocks of different sizes*
- *busy boxes*
- *rings*
- *shapes*
- *snap beads*
- *telephone*
- *magnifying glass*

MOVING AND COORDINATION
- *bowls and balls*
- *pots and pans*
- *ring stacks*
- *ring toss*

CONTROL OF HANDS, FINGERS
- *blocks made out of fabric, foam, cardboard, and wood*
- *building blocks that fit together*
- *towers that interlock*

UNDERSTANDING CAUSE/EFFECT
- *busy box*
- *dominoes*
- *jack-in-the-box*
- *surprise boxes*

MATCHING: ABLE TO SEE SIMILARITIES/DIFFERENCES
- blocks
- color-matching
  sets and boards
- lotto games
- picture
  dominoes
- rings
- shapes

LEARNING SEQUENCES
- beads and laces
- ring stack
- ring toss
- threading, in and
  out of pegs

CLASSIFICATION: SEEING RELATIONSHIPS BETWEEN OBJECTS
- puzzle pieces
- stacking
  products

LANGUAGE IMPROVEMENT
- books
- flashlights
- mirrors
- pictures
- puppets
- puzzles
- tapes

COORDINATION: RHYTHM INSTRUMENTS
- bells
- cymbals
- drums
- maracas
- sticks
- tambourines
- triangles
- xylophones

## Computer Learning

Software allows a child to move at his own pace. Select a product like Edmark's Kid Desk at first, to allow all members of the family to have access to the computer. There exist special keyboards with large keys in bright colors. One example is Intellikeys, a flat keyboard that can be programmed any way that you want. Use the guidelines on page 161 in making your software selection.

# CHECKLIST OF TOYS AND PRODUCTS FOR CHILDREN WITH SPECIAL NEEDS

action figures
activity center
activity mat
art materials
balls
beads
beanbags
blocks
board games
books
bop bag
bubble pipe or
  wand
busy box
checkers
climbing figures
computer software
construction sets
costumes
dolls
dominoes

electronic games
gym
jack-in-the-box
lacing toys
lotto games
magnetic letters
metal frames and
  beads on base
mirror
mobile
Mr. and Mrs. Potato
  Head
musical toys
paper and crayons
Peg-Boards
play dishes
play sets
play tools
plush toys
puppets

push-pull toys
puzzles
rattles
road signs
  (miniatures)
rocking horse
scooter board
See and Say
shape sorters
snap beads
soft toys
stacking ring
swing
tapes
telephone
tricycles
tunnel
videos
wagon
windup toys

# RESOURCES TO ASSIST YOU

The more your special child is involved in play, the happier he is, and the less frustrated or isolated. The Special Olympics program grew out of the commitment of the Joseph P. Kennedy Jr. Foundation in Washington, D.C., to help all children who are afflicted with mental retardation. The foundation is dedicated to helping these children accomplish more, be better coordinated, and have fun in competition.

Check such organizations for books and resources covering the basic information you need for your child's disability. A partial listing follows:

| | |
|---|---|
| Alexander Graham Bell Association for the Deaf | 202-337-5220 |
| American Foundation for the Blind | 800-AFB-LINE |
| American Society for Deaf Children | 800-942-2732 |
| American Speech-Language-Hearing Association | 800-638-8255 |
| Association for Children and Adults with Attention Deficit Disorders | 800-233-4050 |
| (ARC) Association for Retarded Citizens | 817-261-6003 |
| Autism Society of America | 800-328-8476 |
| Council for Exceptional Children | 703-620-3660 |
| Epilepsy Foundation of America | 800-332-1000 |
| Joseph P. Kennedy Jr. Foundation/Special Olympics International | 202-393-1250 |
| Muscular Dystrophy Association | 602-529-2000 |
| National Captioning Institute | 703-917-7600 |
| National Center for Learning Disabilities | 212-545-7510 |
| The National Center for Stuttering | 212-532-1460 |
| National Down's Syndrome Society | 800-221-4602 |
| National Easter Seal Society | 800-221-6827 |
| National Information Center for Children and Youth with Disabilities | 800-695-0285 |
| National Lekotek Center | 800-366-7529 |
| Self Help for Hard of Hearing People | 301-657-2248 |
| United Cerebral Palsy | 800-872-5827 |

# EIGHT

# Play Everywhere

From babyhood your child should play both inside and out-of-doors. The benefits of outdoor play are great: increased health, fresh air, sunshine, and the stimulation of the outer world which broadens his experience and curiosity.

## CREATING A PLAYGROUND

If you have the space you may want to erect playground equipment in your own yard. Certainly wherever your child plays out-of-doors should be safe, challenging, and fun. Use the ideas here to evaluate any play area whether at a child-care center, school, or recreation center. If your community does not have a child's play park, you may want to to join other parents and other interested citizens in the community to create one. There can be no finer investment than in the health and well-being of children.

Parents, working together, can build a sturdy playground in a park or empty lot near their homes for which they have zoning permits, and approval in writing from the owner of record, and of course, the appropriate liability insurance. Research (and, if possible, visit) some of the remarkably innovative child parks in other areas.

A good reference book for this project is by Joan Jeremy and Jay Beckwith, *Build Your Own Playground*. The authors point out that a playground need not be a sterile layout of asphalt, slides, and swings. Jeremy and Beckwith describe how to create a play area which reflects a child's ideal. Topics covered include building materials, division of labor during construction, and establishing playing areas for children with special needs.

The space created should offer safety, security, a variety of playthings, places to sit, and should be easily accessible to child-accommodating restrooms.

Include a secure place for toys to be stored; a place for water, sand, and digging; and a safe place for the use of tricycles, bike-parking, and even roller skating. Don't forget shade, benches, and if possible, a few tables for alfresco parties. This park could be a great place to hold birthday parties.

Materials for the project often are obtainable for free or very inexpensively. Scrounging can be developed into a high art; a play-ground has great potential for creative use of surplus materials. Some likely sources of interesting and inexpensive supplies are:

DISCOUNTED ITEMS:
- Government surplus
- Salvage stores
- Scrap-metal dealers
- State and federal surplus outlets (which often have catalogs)
- Utility companies

POSSIBLE FREEBIES:
- From builders who are clearing sites
- Telephone poles (also short end pieces from the power and telephone companies)
- Tires (all sizes, from surplus tire dealers)

- Trees (from park- or highway-department prunings/transplant-ings)
- Wooden wire reels

## Innovative Applications of Other Surplus

1. Straw and hay: from local fields in the fall, or from a feed store.
   PURPOSE: For jumping in, or using for a thatched roof.
2. Railroad ties*: from railroad companies and crews.
   PURPOSE: for an imbedded balance beam, the sides of a sandbox, a make-believe car with a mounted steering wheel, or a garden enclosure.
3. Large rocks: from road construction sites, gravel pits, or the woods.
   PURPOSE: for damming up a stream to make a pool or stepping stones.
4. Bricks: seconds from a brickyard or construction company.
   PURPOSE: for building forts and constructing a climbing wall.
5. Concrete pipes: from concrete companies or the telephone company.
   PURPOSE: for making tunnels and bridges. Be sure they are well embedded in the ground.
6. Tree sections and tree trunks with limbs: from the city electric company, neighbors, or a lumber mill.
   PURPOSE: for climbing and practicing hammering, sawing, and other woodworking skills.
7. Sand: from the beach, a construction company, or a sand and gravel pit.
   PURPOSE: for making a sandbox. Should have drainage bricks underneath and a cover to keep out cats and dogs.
8. Wooden blocks and pieces of lumber: discards from lumber companies and the city utility company.

*Note: be sure wood is well-sanded with no rough edges

PURPOSE: for building structures with hammers and nails, for stacking and other structures.

9. Ropes, rope ladders, and cargo nets: from hardware stores and shipyards.
   PURPOSE: for climbing and swinging.

10. Barrels: from a hardware store or a distillery.
    PURPOSE: for rolling in, making houses and tunnels. Be sure to sand away any splinters.

11. Large, wooden electric wire spools: from the electric company.
    PURPOSE: for making tables, stools.

12. Discarded rowboat: ask around piers and docks.
    PURPOSE: for imaginary voyages. Drill holes for drainage and use as a sandbox.

13. Automobile tires: from auto junk yards and service stations.
    PURPOSE: Clean them up and paint them bright colors with paint made especially for rubber. Use to roll, to stack, to climb on, and as swings.

## Suggested Outdoor Play Equipment

Balls
Bicycles
Boats
Bricks
Garden supplies
Hammock(s)
Homemade blocks and
   lumber
Homemade wooden boxes
Pails and shovels
Skates (with some obstacles
   to skate over and under)
Sleds (depending on
   weather and hills, of
   course)
Swings (try a variety of
   types)
Tricycles
Tubs (for water, sand, dirt,
   and flowers)
Wheelbarrows
Wooden ladders (for an
   obstacle course)

Please share with Dr. Toy your experiences of building an adventure playground by writing and sending in photos or by e-mailing us, especially if you have created a new place or improved an existing place from any ideas described here. (See resources section for my address.)

## PLAYING AT SCHOOL

When you visit your child's nursery school, child-care center, or school, be sure to look at the condition, supply, and quality of playthings and equipment.

Ask yourself these questions about your child's play space:

1. Are the toys in good working order?
2. Are there enough toys?
3. Is there a good variety of toys appropriate for the child's age and interest?
4. Are the toys easily accessible for the child?
5. Are there adequate indoor and outdoor play areas, with sufficient equipment in both?
6. Do the teachers offer appropriate and challenging activities for the children's playtime?
7. Do the children have time to explore their own interests?
8. Can children bring toys to school from home?
9. Are toys available to both boys and girls?
10. Are the toys appropriate for the children's ages and interests?
11. Do the toys reflect the educational, creative, and active needs of the child?

If the classroom or care center your child is in does not have these items in sufficient quantity and good variety, you and a group of parents may want to provide them:

| | | |
|---|---|---|
| Animals* | Craft materials | Record and tape |
| Art supplies | Dirt, sand, water play | player |
| Balls | Dolls | Ring toss |
| Blocks | Dramatic play items | Rocking chair |
| Bop bag (pop-up) | Hoops | Steps |
| Books | Magazines | Trains, cars, boats |
| Boxes | Plants/vegetables | Tricycles |
| Climbing | Punching bag | Used tires |
| equipment | | |

The preschool should have areas that allow for specific activities that encourage play, such as:

Active tumbling and
   jumping (mattresses,
   bouncers, carpet)
Cooking
Dress-up clothes and props
Gardening
Housecleaning
Library and/or reading
   area

Music: (various instruments
   to play and listen to
   music)
Pets (if there is space and
   interest in caring for
   them)
Quiet (for rest, time-out,
   looking, thinking)

# TRAVEL AND PLAY

Seeing her community and going into a larger world is always an adventure for a young child. Car trips, plane trips, new cities and destinations enrich their lives immensely. It's good to read about

---

*Animals must be properly protected, cared for, and taken home on weekends.

a place, but actually going there is something else! Seeing the sights and smelling the smells are more effective in learning than any other experience.

## The Golden Word Is Preplanning!

For parents who do not do serious advance planning, these adventures can easily turn into catastrophes. If you are headed for a vacation and are going to be spending time in a hotel, do not make reservations until you check out the facilities available for children and the child-enrichment activities the resort offers.

When planning your trip, involve the children. Their excitement can build your own anticipation of the trip and make the preplanning fun for the whole family. They can even learn to read the map of the trip or keep a written journal in a special "Travel Book" (the kind with attractive covers and blank lined pages), or maybe an oral journal on a tape recorder. Dr. Toy recommends you locate at your public library or bookstore books regarding your destination to the child. It will help to make the trip more interesting and informative.

## The Travel Play Bag

Children easily become restless during long or short trips, so plan activities to keep them busy. Before leaving home, show your child how to put together a "Travel Play Bag" to take along: a small backpack, bag, or tote that fits under a seat or in an overhead carrier. They should include items of their own choice like:

ART SUPPLIES:
Crayons
Do-A-Dot-Busy
 Board
Glue sticks
Magazine pictures
Paper
Pens
Safety scissors
Scotch tape
GAMES:
Books of car
 games
Chalkboard
Colorforms play
 sets

Coloring and joke
 books
Coloring cards
Etch-A-Sketch
MAD LIBS
Magnadoodle
Magnetic games
Origami
Pack'n'Go
Paper dolls
Pocket games (chess,
 checkers)
Pocket Simon
Ticktacktoe
Travel Agravation
Travel Bingo

OTHER:
Books
Cassettes (stories,
 music blank tapes)
Puzzles
Stuffed toy (*one!*)
Tape player with
 earphones

Check out books by Rand McNally for travel activities, and a book by Story Evans and Lise O'Haire entitled *Travelmates: Fun Games Kids Can Play in the Car or on the Go*, (Crown), which is filled with games that need no materials. Also check Dr. Toy's Web site (http://www.drtoy.com) for the latest products that provide travel fun.

## Up in the Air Junior Birdmen . . .

Some airlines provide travel packs for children, offering coloring books and crayons, games, and sometimes pilot's wings. But to be sure, take along a set of materials in the Travel Play Bag. When making reservations, arrange beforehand for the special meal you know your child will prefer or bring along some snacks he will enjoy such as granola bars, crackers, or fruit. Milk and soft drinks are served but usually not until the plane is well under-way. Good to take along some bottled water for thirst.

 After the seat belt is fastened your youngster may forage for items from the Travel Play Bag. The onboard movie is seldom something your young child will want to see, but she will, however, enjoy the taped stories and books in her trip bag, or tucked away by you as a surprise. Your offspring keeps cheerfully busy while you relax during the flight.

## Hey, Dad! We're There!

Larger cities offer cultural attractions (many have a children's museum, aquarium, or science discovery center they will be interested in), and most tourist enclaves feature specialty restaurants, sightseeing, and unique shops. Beach resorts provide boating, swimming, and (it is to be hoped) sun. Mountain and country areas offer skiing, skating, hiking, swimming, and nature walks.

No matter where you go with your child, however, he will get tired, hungry, sleepy, and bored. Many good resort hotels provide special products and services for children such as:

- Bicycles and strollers.
- Child-play areas with child-size furniture and playthings.
- Kids' menus—good to arrange ahead of time if needed.
- Lists with child-oriented events in the area: plays and shows, attractions, exhibits, and in many places, great children's museums.
- Programs with crafts, fishing, or snorkling demonstrations.
- Special sightseeing information.

If a circus is in town, the young traveler will be the first to know. Within minutes of registering at the hotel, you can often obtain a free stroller, videotape, or stuffed toy from the hotel by simply calling room service. Some resorts provide a special activities director to take children on sightseeing or field trips. Your child enlarges his information base and his Play Tutors have a reenergizing time-out.

The locale's Visitor Center or Chamber of Commerce can provide a wealth of material on excursions, maps, particular places to go, and things to do, especially about shopping, boutiques, handmade crafts and art by local artisans, and factory outlets.

Early in the trip, before distractions make it difficult, help your child write postcards to grandparents and friends. In the lobby you might allow your child to select a few good souvenirs; make it an occasion to subtly teach quality and value. Inexpensive cameras made especially for children will captivate most kids during and after the trip, and may even lead to a new hobby.

## More on Travel Play
Create games for children to play:

1. One-of-a-kind pictures: Cut pictures from magazines for your children to arrange and paste down in a new picture collage.
2. Hidden newspaper words: Each player has the same newspaper to find words that identify subjects, such as people, money, jobs, seasons, or other topics.
3. Object hunt: Make a list of objects children can locate on the trip. As they see them they can check them off.
4. Make a puzzle: Have children draw a picture. Cut it into four or five parts, then have the children exchange parts and reassemble them.

# CREATIVE PLAY AT HOME

Play is how children learn about life, and toys are tools of play. The rest of this chapter gives you information about potentials for home play. Inventories of items for creative pursuits are provided.

Found and scrounged materials are used every day in classrooms by creative teachers. Similar suggestions follow. In addition to lists of free or inexpensive materials and where to get them, suggested props for role-playing an automobile repairman, forest ranger, beautician, or plumber are given along with ideas for other jobs to explore. Children become aware of the community and people's careers through acting out in free-form play.

## Suggested Scrap Materials for Making Toys at Home or School.

- Art supplies such as acetate, cellophane, clay, and paint.
- Building supplies such as bolts, bricks, Masonite, nails, pipes, screws and wood scraps.
- Clothing items like belts, buckles, gloves, hats, jewelry, lacing, neckties, and socks.
- Containers like egg cartons, gift boxes, hatboxes, ice cream and milk containers, plastic tubs, and shoe boxes.
- Fabric scraps, like burlap, canvas, cotton, denim, drapery, felt, leather, oilcloth, and velvet.
- Grooming aids such as bobby pins and curlers,
- Household items like bottle caps, carpet scraps, clock parts, clothespins, cord, corn starch, eggshells, floor coverings, flour, hangers, inner tubes, lamp shades, linoleum, liquid starch, ornaments, packing materials, pot scrubbers, spaghetti, ribbon, rope, rubber bands, mirrors, picture frames, pipe cleaners, tacks, tiles, and tires.
- Household supplies such as aluminum foil, bottles (non-breakable) cords, foam, grocery bags, hangers, milk cartons, mirrors, pie plates, plastic wrap, string, Styrofoam, and tape.
- Natural materials like acorns, beans, corks, corn husks, driftwood, fruit, gourds, leaves, rocks, sand, seashells, seeds, sponges, and twigs.
- Paper supplies like cardboard, cardboard rollers, construction paper, doilies, greeting cards, magazines, newspapers, paper cups, paper napkins, paper plates, paper towels, paper tubes, sandpaper, shelf paper, spools, straws, wax paper, and wrapping paper.

# SOURCES FOR FREE AND INEXPENSIVE MATERIALS

- Contractors: lumber, tiles, linoleum, wallpaper, pipes, wire.
- Department stores: fabric swatches, rug swatches, corrugated packing cardboard.
- Electric power company: wire, large spools for tables, assorted packing material.
- Garment factories: yarns, buttons, decorative tape, fabric.
- Hardware stores: sample wallpaper books, sample tile charts, linoleum samples.
- Junkyards: unlimited possibilities including clocks, radios, fans, irons, toasters, hinges, handles, and fittings.
- Metal spinning or fabrication companies: scrap pieces.
- Paper companies: unusual kinds of paper, samples, cut ends, damaged sheets, and cardboard.
- Phone company: excess colored wire, spools.
- Plumbers: wires, pipes, tile scraps, linoleum.
- Rug companies: sample swatches, end pieces from rugs cut to size.
- Supermarkets: cartons, packing materials, fruit crates, materials from displays, cardboard display racks.
- Tile and ceramic companies: tiles by the pound (inexpensive) and broken pieces.

# SUGGESTED USES FOR FREE AND INEXPENSIVE MATERIALS

- Playground: large cartons, fruit crates, barrels, concrete blocks, bricks, large stones, spools, ladders, sewage pipe, ropes, bicycle tires, sawhorses, tree trunks, planks, wooden clubhouse, and targets.
- Dramatic play: old clothes; hats; shoes; shawls; beads; jewelry; material to be used as saris; capes and togas; pans; glasses;

gloves; handbags; wallets; aprons; white coats for professionals (doctors); hand mirrors; compacts; long mirrors; old televisions; radios; record players, telephones, irons, and toasters; brooms; dustpans; brushes; tubs; fruit and vegetable crates; sawhorses; baskets; grocery carts; shopping bags; and play money.

• Sand and water play: plastic jugs, bottles, cups, old teapots, coffeepots, watering cans, garden hoses, bottles, tubs, jars with lids, tin cans, wood, cork, shells, sponges, Styrofoam, marbles, rubber balls, balloons, bubble pipes, hand towels, mops, aprons, safe food coloring, soap, flour, wire, string, rubber bands.

• Construction, sewing, woodworking: boxes of all kinds; egg cartons; milk cartons; cookie trays; vegetable cartons; match boxes; plastic bottles; boxes, and jugs; cardboard tubing from paper towels and toilet tissue; broom handles; spools; bottle caps; lids; pipe cleaners; white glue; paste; Scotch tape; masking tape; paper clips; staples; string; rope; wire; brass paper fasteners; wheels and gears from clocks, fans, and cars; handles, knobs, and hinges; scrap wood, nuts, bolts, nails, washers, screws; cloth of various textures and colors (silk, lace, nylon, net, corduroy, wool, velvet, burlap, felt, cotton, yarn, ribbon, rickrack), and sewing accessories (thread, buttons, beads, snaps, buckles, zippers, needles, pins, knitting needles).

• Collage tray: yarn, thread, ribbon, lace, stones, shells, bottle caps, broom straws, straws, toothpicks, pipe cleaners, twigs, fabric, scrap paper, wood chips, feathers, sawdust, sand, macaroni, rice, packing paper, beads, sequins, buttons, foam rubber, cork, scrap rubber, cake paints, seaweed, leaves, pine needles, seeds, chalk, wire, string, white glue, rubber cement.

• Painting: muffin tins, empty plastic squeeze bottles, jars with lids, tin cans, sheets of plastic, newspaper, aprons, sponges, string, straws, sticks, twigs, toothpicks to be used as brushes, wax, liquid starch, and rope clothesline and pins for hanging artwork.

**PLAY POINT:**
Children have fun with a cardboard box and their imagination. Allow your child plenty of time to discover her own inner resources using props.

- Graphics: tin cans, cardboard tubing, rolling pins, pencils, hair curlers, candles to be used as rollers in printing, forks, spoons, knives, potato mashers, buttons, corks, jar lids, blocks, clay, corrugated board, vegetables, rubber bands, paper clips, string, and fabric.
- Clay work: plastic bags and covered tins for storage, plastic material, tools for modeling—pencils, feathers, twigs, forks, knives, spoons, rolling pins, pebbles, shells, leaves, and toothpicks.
- Sculpture scrap: wood and cardboard, string, wire, nails, toothpicks, pipe cleaners, straws, sticks, tin foil, assorted paper, and white glue.

Don't forget the fun of water play, bubbles, and bubble pipes for practicing breath control; blocks for coordination and building; play dishes and pots and pans for practice tea parties; road signs you can make for outdoor play; magnetic letters on the refrigerator to help child recognize letters and words; checkers for learning rules and having fun; and notebooks for writing and sketching.

## Role-Playing: Imagine!

Find props and let play begin. Childhood is filled with the experiences of imagination and role-playing. This is the time to try out occupations without limitations. The more the merrier. Finding out what different people do is the job of childhood.

## FOR THE AUTOMOBILE REPAIRMAN:

Air pump
Automobile-supply
    catalogs
Cable set
Cap or visor
Carburetors
Empty oil cans
Filters

Flashlight
Gears
Gloves
Hammers
Key carrier and
    keys
Oil funnel
Old shirts

Pliers
Rags
Screwdriver
Spark plugs
Used motor parts
Windshield
    wipers
Wiring

## FOR THE FOREST RANGER:

Binoculars
Canteen
Canvas for tent
Compass
Flashlight

Food supplies
Hat
Knapsack
Mess kit
Mosquito netting

Nature books
Rope
Sleeping bag
Small logs

## FOR THE BEAUTICIAN:

Aprons/big bibs
Brushes
Combs
Curlers
Dryer

Emery boards
Empty shampoo
    bottles (plastic)
Hairnets
Hairpins
Magazines

Mirror
Money
Plastic bins
Pencil and paper
Towels

## FOR THE PLUMBER:

Hardware-supply catalog
Hose and nozzles
Measuring devices

Old shirt, cap
Pipes
Plunger

Spade
Spigots
Tools

## OTHER OCCUPATIONS YOUR CHILD MAY WANT TO PLAY:

*Imagine! What* props *will you need for these?*

| | | |
|---|---|---|
| Astronaut | Magician | Reporter |
| Bus driver | Martian | Scientist |
| Doctor | Nurse | Seamstress |
| Electrician | Office worker | Secretary |
| Fireman | Painter | Ship captain |
| Fisherman | Peace Corps worker | Shoe salesman |
| Flight attendant | Pilot | Teacher |
| Frogman | Police officer | Telephone repairman |
| Grocer | Postal worker | Veterinarian |
| | Railway engineer | |

Playing store for example can begin with an orange crate, a box, some fruits and vegetables, and a basket. It's amazing to listen to the creativity of the children using props and their experiences. Or if the child wants to play doctor there can be a stethoscope, tongue depresser, Q-Tip, Band-Aids, table and chair, and a sick teddy bear.

Your child may want to open a flower shop, pet store, bank, shoe store, or dress shop. He may want to learn to be a different entrepreneur every day. Or she may want to become the driver of an airplane, boat, bus, dump truck, train, or tugboat. Encourage your child as he dreams and acts out ideas for fun-filled hours. Of course, reading books about careers of others will only add to her information and understanding.

# PLAY IS ALL AROUND YOU!

As Play Tutor, challenge your imagination to locate "props" and costumes that work well with each role. Prepare your child by talking with him about the parts he wants to act out. If he makes mistakes about his role, or if he says something unintentionally hilarious during the play, remember, never laugh *at* him. If *she* realizes she's been funny and laughs at herself, join in with the laughter gently and with love.

Play is all around you! Find innovative ways for your youngster to play. Have fun with your child. The results are well worth the time and effort.

Remember those early memories you had? This is the time memories are made for your child. Make the most of them!

Here are some recommended ideas to create great experiences to enrich your child's PQ.

## PLAY IDEAS: 160 SUGGESTED ACTIVITIES TO DO WITH YOUR CHILD

Never be at a loss as to what to do with your child to have fun. Choose from any of the following kidpowered activities that help build your child's "PQ":

1. Action-figure play
2. Airplane making
3. Archery
4. Art
5. Audio tapes
6. Auto racing /miniature cars
7. Baking
8. Ball throwing
9. Banner making
10. Basketball
11. Baton twirling
12. Bead making
13. Beanbag games
14. Biking
15. Binocular viewing
16. Bird watching

17. Block building
18. Board games
19. Boat sailing
20. Book reading
21. Boomerang
22. Bowling
23. Bubble blowing
24. Bug collecting
25. Butterfly watching
26. Calligraphy
27. Candle making
28. Card games
29. Carpentry
30. Cartooning
31. Chalk designs
32. Checkers
33. Chemistry set
34. Chess
35. Clay modeling
36. Collage
37. Coloring book
38. Computer games
39. Computer instruction
40. Computer software
41. Construction toys
42. Cookie making
43. Cooking
44. Costume making
45. Crafts
46. Dancing
47. Decoupage
48. Doll clothes making
49. Dollhouse decorating
50. Doll making
51. Dominoes
52. Drumming
53. Exercise

54. Face-painting
55. Finger-painting
56. Flower making
57. Frisbee throwing
58. Games
59. Gardening
60. Greeting-card design
61. Guitar playing
62. Gyroscope
63. Harmonica
64. Hiking
65. Horseshoes
66. Internet exploration
67. Jewelry making
68. Juggling
69. Jump rope
70. Kaleidoscope
71. Kite making/flying
72. Knitting
73. Knot tying
74. Letter writing
75. Lifting
76. Listening
77. Magic tricks
78. Magnets
79. Magnifying-glass study
80. Making musical instruments
81. Marbles
82. Marionette play
83. Mask making
84. Microscope
85. Mobile making
86. Model making
87. Mosaic crafts
88. Music making
89. Nature study
90. Nature walks

91. Needlepoint
92. Origami
93. Ornament making
94. Paper dolls
95. Paper making
96. Papier-mâché
97. Photography
98. Piano study
99. Ping-Pong
100. Pinwheel
101. Play store
102. Pool
103. Poster making
104. Puppets and puppet theater
105. Puzzles
106. Quilting
107. Radio-control cars
108. Reading
109. Ring toss
110. Rope tying
111. Robot play
112. Rowing
113. Sailing
114. Sand play
115. Sand sculpture
116. Science experiments
117. Scrapbook
118. Sewing
119. Ship model
120. Silk screening
121. Skating
122. Sketching
123. Skiing
124. Sledding
125. Soap making
126. Soap sculpture
127. Stained-glass making

128. Stamp collecting
129. Stamp crafts
130. Stationery design
131. Sticker fun
132. String art
133. Swimming
134. Tapes
135. Tea party
136. Telescope viewing
137. Terrarium
138. Tops
139. Trading-card swap
140. Trains and train layouts
141. Travel games
142. Ukulele
143. Velocipede
144. Video games
145. Videotapes
146. Violin study
147. Volleyball
148. Walkie-talkie
149. Walking
150. Water colors
151. Weaving
152. Whistling
153. Writing in a diary
154. Writing poems
155. Writing stories
156. Xylophone
157. Yarn crafts
158. Yoga
159. Yo-yo
160. Zoo trek

Let us know if we left out something that is fun and educational.

# NINE

# Play Power

There are many ongoing and, in some cases, very active controversies surrounding toys. Over the years, issues have included sexism, violence, and consumerism. To date no conclusions have been reached, no long-range or effective action taken.

I will respond to these controversies and offer my opinion on some of these issues, but I am also interested in knowing what you think of the topics, so please write me and let me know your views.

## Sexism

Some toys and packages seem to be directed solely at girls, others seem to consciously exclude them. Manufacturers have made assumptions based on what they think children want to play with rather than researching the matter adequately. Some have not kept up with the changing attitudes in the '80s and '90s. Others, perhaps, are run by policy setters who still subscribe to a 1950s worldview.

This narrow thinking separates girls and boys and excludes each from sharing in the same sorts of activities. Few dolls, for example, are made that appeal to boys. And although inroads have been made on behalf of girls (many of whom like action figures or the basketball hoop above the garage door), this is not due to manufacturer accommodation, but to parental wisdom. Some companies are investing in girls-oriented software to appeal to their interests and to help them improve their use of the computer. These are products that can begin to make a difference. However, many specific products are specifically designed for one sex. Children may however select what brings the greatest connection to their interests at a particular time.

If a child does not have experience with certain kinds of play in childhood—for example, like failing to learn to roller or ice skate—it gets harder to learn later. To be fair to both boys and girls it is urged that you offer, and let them play with, all sorts of playthings. Let them make their decisions based on their own inclinations.

## Violence

Violence is perceived by children in many forms. The debate about V-chips or control of the television, the movies, or the on-line system and the messages that come through the media every day says something rather unpleasant about our society that words alone do not. Toys and play do reflect the issues of our culture.

Our society is at a critical stage, a choice, first and foremost, that either we must involve ourselves in making things work for everyone or, by a laissez-faire attitude, allow things to be frustrating, fearful, and frightening for us all.

We can choose the toys, games, programs, movies, and experiences we provide our children. We can choose what we do in our community to improve things for other youngsters, especially those who do not have the same enriched environment as ours.

Children who are deprived because they are not loved or cared about, who are not fed properly, not receiving proper and timely medical care, are more likely to act out negatively and hurt themselves and others both now and in the future.

We must be concerned that our own children learn to share, to give to others, and to curb their tendency to play with violence in any form. We do what we must to instill those same values in deprived kids. This can be done in myriad ways, although the best is working one on one with such a child. Not all of us can do this. But we can support those who do, as behind-the-scenes volunteers (i.e., reading aloud, devising games for small groups) or even financially.

We have to accept that there is a fork in the road: either we do nothing about society's tumble into even greater violence, or we take a hand to curb it and change things for the better. It can happen through a sea change in the media.

If media officials would care about the whole of society instead of profits, advertising income, and exploitation of the worst in us all, and began to think instead of how to create programming for and about people that educates and inspires, it would make a difference.

Studies indicate that we, the audience, are responsible for the programming, and it is we who turned off *Highway to Heaven* to watch *Rocky* or *Rambo* on another channel. What are we going to do differently? For one thing, some activists boycott the advertisers and programs that promote violence. It is hard to believe that those who prefer violence outnumber those of us who don't. Parents who care must speak up, and speak out.

There are stories of children who do good things for themselves and others; people who overcome great odds to become winners; teens who get busy with constructive activities instead of negative exploits; adults who show respect for each other and try to learn about the differences between people, only to find that everyone is really very much alike—good and bad in a mix we're ever trying to improve. If we all worked at it, the world around us could shift dramatically in less than one generation.

## Consumerism

The continuous bombardment by the media, especially television, influences children to demand advertised products. It's pervasive, well-planned, and well-financed. A few toys always get the "big hype" every year and make a lot of money for the company and the shareholders. Unfortunately, because of this media blitz, too many children feel deprived when they do not get the BIG one. It matters little if it's Elmo, Barbie, or Cabbage Patch, when the push-and-panic-to-buy button is on, it causes many strange and bizarre behaviors.

Around the holiday season, some parents actually get violent with each other in toy stores, fighting over a single Nintendo or the one Tickle Me that is left. Whether it is a vibrating stuffed animal or a Turbo-Man, it's the behavior and the resulting feeling of being "in" or "out" during what is supposed to be a spiritual holiday of sharing that is so incredibly demeaning.

Why should any child feel deprived when there are thousands of wonderful, upbeat toys that are truly educational, valuable, and full of fun? How can our families become so worked up over getting one item and forget all the rest of the toys at home? Is this what we want to express to our children?

When these times of extreme consumerism hit, it might be a good idea to pause and think again about the meaning of giving and receiving. Ralph Waldo Emerson's essay on gifts is a provocative and entertaining read on the subject.

Gifts historically go hand in hand with holidays of spiritual significance. Perhaps the true meaning of the holiday season is revealed by the special time we spend with our children, going to church, taking a walk in the woods, finding a surprise—a giving with joy, a taking with exhilaration. And the sharing of love among dad, mom, and kids.

## Consider Action

If all the children who do not have toys were given a few, their new world of wonder would start with no longer feeling left out . . .

If their parents were helped to earn, learn, and turn into contributing members of the community, their new world would give them self-esteem and strength . . .

If seniors could help youngsters to read, and give them some of the attention and love they need, when they both might otherwise feel neglected and alone . . .

If schools provided wholesome after-school activities so all children were safe until their parents were finished with work . . .

We could, one by one, change the lives and the spirits of ourselves and others for the better.

Smart Play is integral to a child's life. But, if children cannot play safely after school or productively at home, what choices remain? Coming home to an empty house, watching TV alone at home, is not a nurturing experience.

There are far too many families facing these problems in every community, but they can be resolved if we adults are able to bring to the challenge the same smarts, energy, and single-minded drive that we bring to our careers.

If, each and every day, we do not show our children that we value and love them, where will they learn that they matter to us?

Something to think about.

# WHY NOT COMMUNITY PLAY CENTERS?

Children always need safe places to play. I would like to see every community create Community Play Centers in or near the schools to develop learning, physical activity, and creativity. The facilities would include computer and board games that teach children needed skills and strategy, arts, crafts, music, theater, dance, and reading. Tie in the idea of creative outdoor play with space for a creative adventure play yard and children will spend many hours happily engaged in positive and productive play.

Usage of the center would be scheduled by age or aptitude group, so that youngsters with similar abilities could share activities. In turn children would have supervised play outdoors. Add a butterfly garden—flowers that attract butterflies—and you have a perfect blending of natural play and learning. Children will find it fascinating to learn about the flowers and they will if given the opportunity to participate in planting and tending the garden. If given a chance children can be players and productive members of the community.

The after-school, year-round Community Play Center would provide a supervised environment for children whose parents must work until 5 or 6 P.M. Safe, enriching child care is more a matter of concern to parents than any other factor. The Play Center is appropriate not only for younger schoolchildren, but also for those eleven- and twelve-year-olds who are often "latchkey kids," able to survive without direct adult assistance for a limited time, but who receive no guidance for productive play.

Is it any wonder that many children find the community unfriendly? For too long, schools have closed their doors at 3 P.M., and the teaching staff (with a few exceptions) race out of the building to their own pursuits. Many school policies discourage students from remaining on the premises because of liability worries. Yet the school building is one of the perfect locations for a Play Center. Few other buildings in the community can provide the ease and accessibility. Perhaps we need to reexamine the real purpose of the community school and find new ways to extend its value year round.

There are a few recreation centers like those described, but only limited numbers of children are able to attend these programs due to the distance they have to travel to reach them.

If the idea appeals to you, talk to neighbors, friends, and other parents about the local need, and the advantages not just to school children, but to adults with no child in the home, as it is to their advantage not to have unsupervised children in the neighborhood. Then, with everyone's backing, group members can campaign appropriate civic authorities and school districts. Grants for the project, federal or private, are worth exploring.

Certainly children need play as a natural part of their everyday lives. Providing a Play Center as part of the community will go a long way to giving children what they need—safe play experiences. It would benefit everyone in the community, with new jobs for talented adults and college students in training to work with children, and assure that children will be protected, nurtured, and respected.

# VALUE OF THE BOOK

Sharing the information in this book has been valuable to me. Putting it together has been hard work, but I've had the chance to: bring together experience and facts, appreciate the data now available on child growth and development, convey the research on play and toys, and report on all the wonderful products that are being made.

Perhaps best and foremost, this book lets me share with parents ideas that will enrich the play of all of the great children everywhere, producing happy, well-adjusted, productive, successful adults of the future who, too, will play with their children.

I have always been fascinated with playthings. From my earliest memories as a child playing with self-created clothespin dolls, cardboard boxes, and listening to the radio during World War II when toys were scarce, my family encouraged play, laughter, games, reading, and physical activity, which were not scarce and also did not cost anything to enjoy. Trips to the library were magical portals to my imagination. Listening to stories on the radio fueled pictures of heroes and heroines. My mother read stories aloud in a special way, changing her voice to match the story, that made reading magical. Those early memories persist as I evaluate the content of tapes, books, and other products. Children want to listen to music, hear stories that share adventure and values, encourage thinking, provide new experiences, and are fun. Indeed, everything the child does in the context of play has lasting benefits and is more easily retained.

This book on play has truly been an important opportunity for me to review and synthesize my studies, experiences, and information about play and playthings. It completes a long process I began many years ago, examining the role and importance of play and the use of toys. Play is powerful. Memories of our earliest play experiences remain vivid. You found that out if you did the memory exercise at the beginning of the book. Perhaps in reading more about play additional memories have surfaced.

As a child-development specialist, observing children at play has been one of my strongest professional pursuits, for through play I make note of and better understand a child's personality, intelligence, creativity, socialization, emotional state, physical coordination, curiosity, and many more aspects. We as professionals and parents need to spend more time observing children at play to comprehend the stages they are currently in, and their unmet needs and issues. When we approach children with this knowledge we can better understand and communicate.

So much of childhood should be about play, enhanced and treasured, but frequently it is not. Play is simply not valued as fully as it should be in our society. Too often children are rushed into other pursuits and are not given the respect, time, or right tools needed for play. Or they are pushed into playing with media-promoted products that may be unsuitable for young, impressionable minds.

Many children simply are not allowed to fully play as much as they need to. Instead of active play with toys and crafts they are too often parked for long periods of time sitting passively in front of an instrument that provides the "show and tell" instead of involving them. Too often they are not allowed to pursue the healthy, active play they continuously need, indoors and out of doors, due to familial restrictions such as parents at work. When TV is used as a baby-sitter, the real experiences and spontaneity of play are turned off.

Unfortunately, society is not always good to children. Many homes, playgrounds, and toys prove to be unsafe. Play takes time. It is a process that cannot be rushed. Discovery, practice, trial and error are all part of the process. Toys fueled with the unlimited imagination of play are magical vessels for building healthy minds and emotions. Those powerful memories of play are retained long into adulthood. They shape us as parents. They influence how we spend our leisure time. They determine how we play with our children.

Adults who themselves have high Play Quotient (PQ, the ability to utilize and maximize play experiences) are more apt to select appropriate toys, help their children learn to play fully, and help their children to heighten their own PQ and thus be happier and more fulfilled. Playful people are less stressed, more inquisitive, more open to new experiences, more creative, and more willing to take risks. Children with high PQ are willing to share their enthusiasm for play with their siblings, friends, and family. They explore all of the possibilities available and are eager for more play experiences.

I hope that this book helped you to better understand how to create a playful environment to enhance your child's total development. I hope that parents will be encouraged to provide many of the basic ingredients that will maximize their child's PQ. Having fun together will reduce stress, improve communications, and build a happier family life.

Toys are more than a multibillion-dollar industry. They can be beacons of light that can help to illuminate and shine on the play experiences of children. When the alignment of designer and man-ufacturer is focused appropriately on the needs of the child, the results can be pure magic. The product may not necessarily be a best-seller, but it can be a product that has value and lasts over time. You still remember the blocks, hoops, marbles, and yo-yos you played with. Even today you smile when you see a child playing with the very same playthings you enjoyed at her age. Toys, after all, reflect our society in all of its different manifesta-tions. Let's play!

# RESOURCES

## CATALOGS, MAGAZINES, AND ORGANIZATIONS

Many fine toys and other children's products for home and school can be obtained through these catalogs, magazines, and service organizations. If you learn of others not included here please let us know. *Thank you!*

## TOYS AND CHILDREN'S PRODUCTS (HOME)

Alcazar Music.....................................800-541-9904
Back to Basics...................................800-356-5360
Bits & Pieces....................................800-544-7297
Brainstorms......................................800-621-7500
Cambridge Educational .........................800-468-4227
Child Craft ......................................800-631-5657
ChildLife.........................................800-467-9464
Chinaberry Book Service .......................800-776-2242
*Classic Toy Trains* .............................800-533-6644
Coalition for Children's Videos ...............800-331-6197
Discovery Toys ..................................800-426-4777
Disney Catalog...................................800-237-5751
Educational Insights............................800-933-3277
Edutainment Catalog............................800-338-3844
Egghead Computer..............................800-344-4323
Family Travel Guides............................510-527-5849
FAO Schwarz ...................................800-426-8697
Great Kids Company ...........................800-533-2166
Hand in Hand...................................800-872-9745
Heartland Music ................................800-727-2233

Heartsong........................................800-325-2502
Hobby House Press............................800-554-1447
Into the Wind..................................800-541-0314
Just for Kids....................................800-899-7666
Kid Safety of America ........................800-524-1156
KidSoft..........................................800-354-6150
Lilly's Kids ......................................800-285-5555
Metropolitan Museum of Art ..................800-468-7386
Music for Little People........................800-727-2233
One Step Ahead................................800-274-8440
PlayFair..........................................800-824-7255
Pleasant Company..............................800-845-0005
Right Start.......................................800-548-8531
School Zone Publishing........................800-253-0564
This Country's Toys............................800-359-6144
TimeLife Education ............................800-449-2010
Toys to Grow On ..............................800-542-8338
Turn Off the TV ..............................800-949-8688
US Committee for UNICEF ..................800-553-1200
US Toy/Constructive Playthings..............800-832-0572
WorldWide Games..............................800-888-0987
Young Explorers ..............................800-239-7577

## TOYS AND CHILDREN'S PRODUCTS (SCHOOL)

ABC School Supply............................800-669-4222
Beckley Cardy Group..........................800-227-1178
Chimetime.......................................800-477-5075
Community Playthings.........................800-777-4244
Gryphon House Books.........................800-638-0928
Holbrook ........................................800-822-8121
JL Hammet......................................800-333-4600
Kaplan School Supply..........................800-334-2014
Learning Resources ............................800-222-3909
Summit Learning................................800-239-7577

## MAGAZINES (CHILDREN)

American Girl ....................................800-234-1278
Baby Bug ........................................800-827-0227
Boys' Life .....................972-580-2088 (also in Braille)
Crayola Kids ....................................800-846-7968
Cricket..........................................800-827-0227
Girls' Life ......................................800-999-3222
Highlights for Children...........................800-255-9517
Kid City.........................................800-678-0613
Kidsoft .........................................800-354-6132
Ladybug.........................................800-827-0227
Nickelodeon Magazine............................515-280-8750
Ranger Rick.....................................800-588-1650
Sesame Street Magazine.........................800-678-0613
Spider ..........................................800-827-0227
Sports Illustrated for Kids ......................888-217-8264
Stone Soup .....................................800-447-4569
3-2-1 Contact...................................800-678-0613
Zillions.........................................800-234-1645

## MAGAZINES (PARENTS/TEACHERS)

Baby Magazine...................................212-986-1422
Child ...........................................800-777-0222
Children's Software Revue.......................800-993-9499
Classic Toy Trains ..............................800-533-0644
Collecting Toys..................................800-446-5489
Creative Classroom .............................800-678-0613
Doll Reader .....................................800-829-3340
Family Life Magazine ...........................800-234-0847
FamilyPC........................................800-413-9749
Gerber Baby Book...............................800-443-7237
Kidscreen .......................................800-543-4512
Michaels Arts & Crafts—Kid's Crafts ...........800-856-8060
Parenting Magazine .............................800-234-0847
Parent's Magazine...............................800-727-3682
Scholastic Parent and Child.....................800-631-1586

*Sesame Street Parents* ........................... 800-678-0613
*Single Mother* .................................... 704-888-6667
*Working Mother Magazine* ...................... 800-234-9675
*Young Children* .................................. 800-424-2460

## ORGANIZATIONS

See additional organizations.
These organizations produce publications, magazines, and other resources for parents and professionals. Please let us know of any useful organizations not listed.

AAA Foundation for Traffic Safety ............ 202-638-5944
American Academy of Pediatrics ............... 847-228-5005
Center for Accessible Technology
(for disabled) ............................... 800-455-7970
Center for Media Education ................... 202-628-2620
Children's Book Council ...................... 212-966-1990
Children's TV Resource and Education Center.... 415-864-8424
Consumer Federation of America ............. 202-387-6121
Family Resource Coalition .................... 312-341-0900
Institute for Childhood Resources ............. 800-551-8697
International Association for the Child's Right
to Play ..................................... 516-463-5176
KidsNet ........................................ 202-291-2400
Lekotek ........................................ 800-366-8697
National Association for the Education of Young
Children .................................... 800-424-2460
National Center for Children &
Youth with Disabilities ..................... 800-695-0285
National Child Care Information Center ....... 800-616-2242
National SAFE KIDS Campaign .............. 202-662-0600
Toy Manufacturers of America ................ 800-851-9955
USA Toy Library Association ................. 847-864-3330
U.S. Consumer Product Safety Commission ... 800-638-2772
U.S. Department of Education/Ntl. Library of
Education .................................... 800-424-1616

## Resources on Toys and Products

Reports on evaluation of products include:

DR. TOY'S GUIDE
on the Internet-http//www.drtoy.com
Current reports available free with a SASE # 10 envelope to:

Dr. Toy
268 Bush St.
San Francisco, CA 94104
415-861-1169

Information on hundreds of award-winning products for children from babies to older children selected by Dr. Toy including Best Vacation, After School, Classic, and the Annual 100 Best Products, plus articles and many other resources. Weekly column, "Dr. Toy," distributed by King Features Syndicate.

Oppenheim Toy Portfolio
40 E. 9th St.
New York, NY 10003
212-598-0502

Review of toys, products, books, and videos. Subscription.

Parent's Choice
Box 185
Waban, MA 012168
617-965-5913

Quarterly report of toys, books, videos, tapes, and computer programs. Subscription.

## ON-LINE

For additional up to date information check links on Dr. Toy's Web site (http://www.drtoy.com).

## ADDITIONAL RESOURCES

For names of speciality/hobby stores nearest you contact:

American Specialty Toy Retailers (ASTRA)...888-303-8697
National Retail Hobby Stores Association .....800-397-8398

## ADDITIONAL TIPS

- Locate the children's museum or art or science museum nearest you and you will find a great place to visit with your child plus a terrific gift shop loaded with great stuff.
- Check the local parenting newspaper in your community for stores, sales, special places, events, information, and other important services for the whole family.
- Visit or call your local child-care referral agency for the latest information on resources in your community.
- Contact the local American Automobile Association for their publications and guides to what's new for the whole family in your area or in the locale you plan to visit.
- Visit or contact the Convention and Visitor's Bureau in your area or in the locale you plan to visit for updates on family resources.
- Contact the YMCA/YWCA or other youth organization in your community for updates on local services for children.
- Visit your local library, the children's section, for books, magazines, and more resources.

# REFERENCES

## CHAPTER ONE: THE IMPORTANCE OF PLAY AND TOYS

Goleman, Daniel. *Emotional Intelligence: Why It Can Matter More Than IQ for Character, Health, and Lifelong Achievement.*
ISBN 0-553-09503-X
New York: Bantam Books, 1995.
352 pgs.
Description of emotional intelligence, literacy, and importance of recognizing them.


Piaget, Jean. *Play, Dreams, and Imitation in Childhood.*
ISBN 0-393-00171-7
New York: W.W. Norton & Co., 1962.
296 pgs.
Technical book on child development.

## CHAPTER TWO: BABY

Eisenberg, Arlene; Murkoff, Heidi E.; Hathaway, Sandee E. *What to Expect the First Year.*
ISBN 0-89480-577-0
New York: Workman Publishing, 1989.
672 pgs.
Infant development, care, addresses both physical and emotional needs of the whole family.

Jones, Sandy; Freitag, Werner. *Guide to Baby Products*, 4th ed.
ISBN 0-89043-713-0
Yonkers, NY: Consumer Reports Books, 1994.
288 pgs.
Up-to-date information on safety, convenience, comfort, and durability.


Lansky, Vicki. Games Babies Play: *From Birth to Twelve Months*.
ISBN 0-916773-33-7
Deephaven, MN: Book Peddlers, 1993.
98 pgs.
Games for infants progress up to one year.

## CHAPTER THREE: TODDLER

Sparling, Joseph; Lewis, Isabelle. *Learning Games for the First Three Years: A Guide to Parent-Child Play*.
ISBN 0-8027-7239-0
New York: Walker, 1984.
226 pgs.
One hundred games, grouped in six-month age spans. Games stress self-image, language, creativity.

## CHAPTER FOUR: PRESCHOOLER

Britton, Lesley. *Montessori Play & Learn: A Parents' Guide to Purposeful Play from Two to Six*.
ISBN 0-517-59182-0
New York: Crown, 1993.
144 pgs.
Activities, games, supplement preschool learning, explains Montessori method and how to use it.

Hamilton, Leslie. *Child's Play Around the World: 170 Crafts Games, and Projects for Two- to Six-Year-Olds.*
ISBN 0-399-52208-5
New York: Perigee, 1996.
224 pgs.
Instructions, drawings, about crafts and games from all over the world.

## CHAPTER FIVE: PRIMARY SCHOOLER

Britz-Crecelius, Heidi. *Children at Play: Using Waldorf Principles to Foster Childhood Development.*
ISBN 0-89281-629-5
Rochester, VT: Inner Traditions, 1996.
135 pgs.
Significance of a child's play in shaping the child's humanity.

*Which Toy for Which Child: A Consumer's Guide for Selecting Suitable Toys, Ages Six Through Twelve.*
Washington, DC: U.S. Consumer Product Safety Commission, 1994.
13 pgs.
Outline of children's abilities and interests, followed by toy lists.

## CHAPTER SIX: OLDER CHILD

Sarquis, Jerry L.; Sarquis, Mickey; Williams, John P. *Teaching Science with Toys: Toy-Based Chemistry Activities for Grades K–9.*
ISBN 1-88-382204-1
Blue Ridge Summit, PA: Terrific Science, 1994.
296 pgs.
Uses ordinary materials to teach chemistry.

## CHAPTER SEVEN: SPECIAL NEEDS

Schwartz, Sue. *The Language of Toys: Teaching Communication Skills to Special-Needs Children.*
ISBN 0-933149-08-5
Rockville, MD: Woodbine House, 1988.
280 pgs.
Shows parents and teachers how to use toys to create activities for language development.

## CHAPTER EIGHT: PLAY EVERYWHERE

Brokaw, Meredith; Gilbar, Annie. *The Penny Whistle Any Day Is a Holiday Party Book.*
ISBN 0-684-80917-6
New York: Fireside, 1996.
*The Penny Whistle Traveling with Kids Book.*
ISBN 0-671-88163-1
New York: Fireside, 1995.
Series of useful seasonal and other activity books.


Evans, Story; O'Haire, Lise. *Travelmates: Fun Games Kids Can Play in the Car or on the Go—No Materials Needed.*
ISBN 0-517-88760-6
New York: Crown, 1997.
95 pp
Easy to follow games for children to play without needing anything else.


Sumners, Carolyn. *Toys in Space: Exploring Science with the Astronauts.*
ISBN 0-07-069489-3
New York: McGraw-Hill, 1997.
Over forty inexpensive toys you can make or obtain with directions to demonstrate principles of science.

Thompson, Susan Conklin. *Natural Materials: Creative Activities for Children.*
ISBN 0-673-36033-4
Glenview, IL: Goodyear, 1993.
185 pgs.
Make unusual toys—cornhusk dolls plus wallpaper, pretzels, and sand paintings.

## CHAPTER NINE: PLAY POWER

Gardner, Howard. *Multiple Intelligences: The Theory in Practice.*
ISBN 0-465-01822-x
New York: Basic Books, 1993.
304 pgs.
Children learn through different styles and adults need to be aware of these styles.

# ALSO BY THE AUTHOR

## BOOKS

*The Alphabet Tree.* Mt. Desert, ME: Windswept House, 1985.

*Choosing Child Care: A Guide for Parents.* San Francisco: Parents and Child Care Resources, 1976.

*Choosing Child Care: A Guide for Parents.* New York: Dutton, 1981.

*Confronting the Child Care Crisis.* Boston: Beacon Press, 1979.

*Creative Centers and Homes,* Vol. 111 *Child Care, A Comprehensive Guide.* New York: Human Sciences Press, 1978.

*Keys to Choosing Child Care.* New York: Barron's, 1991.

*Model Programs and Their Components,* Vol. 11: *Child Care, A Comprehensive Guide.* New York: Human Sciences Press, 1975.

*NVGA Bibliography of Occupational Literature.* Washington, DC: National Vocational Guidance Association, 1963.

*Parents and Child Care: A Report on Child Care Consumers in San Francisco.* San Francisco: Far West Laboratory for Educational Research and Development, 1974.

*Physical Education and Recreation for the Mentally Retarded.* Washington, DC: Joseph P. Kennedy Foundation & Southern Regional Education Board, 1967.

*Rationale for Child Care Services—Programs vs. Politics,* Vol. 1: *Child Care, A Comprehensive Guide.* New York: Human Sciences Press, 1975.

*Special Needs and Services,* Vol. IV: *Child Care, A Comprehensive Guide.* New York: Human Sciences Press, 1979.

*The Toy Chest : A Complete Sourcebook of Toys for Children.* Secaucus, NJ: Lyle Stuart, 1986.

*The Whole Child: A Sourcebook.* New York: Putnam/Perigee, 1981.

## SELECTED ARTICLES AND PUBLICATIONS

"Career Opportunities in the Peace Corps." Washington, DC: Peace Corps, 1963.

*The Children Are Waiting for Child Care.* KQED-TV, San Francisco. Documentary (Written, Produced and Directed ) 1974, 30 minutes.

"Federally Sponsored Child Care." Chapter six in *Child Care: Who Cares?* by Pam Robey. New York: Basic Books, 1972.

"Need for Child Care for Children of Federal Employees." Testimony to Select Subcommittee on Education and Labor, Hearings on Child Care HR 13520. Washington, DC, 1969.

Features on toys by the author have appeared in *Early Childhood News, Family Circle, Parenting Magazine, EdPlay, Playthings Magazine, San Francisco Examiner, San Francisco Chronicle, Working Woman, Detroit Free Press, Toy and Hobby World, Special Report, Children's Business, Four Seasons Magazine, Play Magazine, Image Magazine,* and others.

Features on child care by the author have appeared in *Parenting Magazine, Day Care and Early Education, Young Children, Humanist Magazine,* and others.

NOTE: If number is not correct call Toy Manufacturers of America (212-675-1141). Or check Dr. Toy's Web site (http://www.drtoy.com) or 800 Information Toll-Free Directory (800-555-1212).

ABC Feelings .................................800–745–3170
Accord Publishing ...........................888–333–1676
Ace Novelty .................................800–759–1223
Age Appropriate Puzzles .....................800–961–7756
Albert Whitman ..............................800–255–7675
Alcazar Music ...............................800–541–9904
ALEX ........................................800–666–2539
All Night Media .............................800–782–6733
American Melody .............................800–220–5557
Ampersand Press .............................800–624–4263
Anatex ......................................800–999–9599
Angeles Group ...............................800–346–6313
Animal Wrappers .............................509–447–2907
Anything's Puzzable .........................800–984–8486
Applause ....................................800–777–6990
Are We There Yet? ...........................800–892–9012
Aristoplay ..................................888–478–4263
Basic Fun ...................................800–662–3380
BEKA ........................................888–999–2352
Berkeley Systems ............................510–540–5535
Binary Arts .................................888–789–9538
Binney & Smith/Crayola ......................800–272–9652
Bogner Entertainment ........................310–473–0139

The First Years ...............................800–533–6708
Fisher-Price ..................................800–432–5437
Fiskars .......................................800–950–2988
Flexible Flyer ................................800–521–6233
Folkmanis ....................................800–443–4463
Forecees .....................................616–649–2900
Forte Sports .................................800–305–9453
Frank Schaffer Publications ...................800–421–5565
Free Spirit Publishing ........................800–735–7323
Fresh Tracks .................................800–551–6145
Fujitsu Interactive ...........................888–992–5433
Funopolis ....................................888–386–6765
Future Boomers ..............................800–743–6244
Galoob Toys .................................800–442–5662
Galt Toys ....................................800–899–4258
Gamewright ..................................800–638–7568
Gemini Kaleidoscopes .........................800–999–8700
George F. Cram ..............................800–227–4199
Golden Books ................................800–323–3568
Goodness Sake Products .......................607–272–0294
Good Stuff Corporation .......................718–937–3333
Goodyear Books .............................800–628–4480
Gordon R. Wren .............................602–966–6034
Great American Puzzle Factory ................800–922–1194
Greenleaf Products ...........................800–847–2545
Guidecraft ...................................800–554–6526
Hal Leonard .................................800–524–4425
Hands On Toys ..............................888–442–6376
HarperCollins ...............................212–207–7000
Hartley Courseware ..........................800–801–0040
Hasbro Interactive ...........................800–638–6927
Heartsong Communications ....................800–648–0755
Hero Arts Creative Rubber Stamps .............800–822–4376
High Windy Pete .............................800–637–8679
Holgate Toy Company ........................800–499–1929
Hollow Woodworks ...........................800–383–0247
Hoopla by Andre .............................800–747–2454
Hugg-A-Planet ...............................800–332–7840

Hypergee/Air Pogo .............................800–880–7646
IBM ..............................................800–426–7235
Ideals Publishing ..............................800–327–5113
Imagiix .........................................800–462–4449
Imagination Project ............................888–477–6532
Inspiration Software ...........................800–877–4292
IntelliTools ...................................800–899–6687
International PlayThings ........................800–631–1272
Irwin Toy ......................................800–268–1733
John Wiley & Sons ..............................800–225–5945
Jostens Learning Center Corporation ...........800–247–1380
KAPLA ..........................................888–447–5275
Kenner .........................................800–327–8264
Kidderoo Creative ..............................612–789–2700
Kidpower .......................................800–545–7529
Kidsview .......................................201–445–2101
KikaFlik .......................................908–494–4488
Kimbo Educational ..............................800–631–2187
K'NEX ..........................................800–543–5639
Knowledge Adventure ............................800–542–4240
LEGO DACTA .....................................888–534–6748
LEGO SYSTEM ....................................800–233–8756
Lakeshore Learning Materials ...................800–421–5354
Latz Chance Games ..............................770–579–6173
Lauri ..........................................800–451–0520
Lawrence Productions ...........................800–421–4157
Leap Frog ......................................800–701–5327
Learning Curve Toys ............................800–704–8697
Learning Materials Workshop ....................800–693–7164
Learning Passport ..............................800–853–2762
Learning Products ..............................314–997–6400
Learning Resources .............................800–222–3909
Leeko Industries ...............................800–938–1915
LGB of America .................................800–669–0607
Liqui-Mark .....................................800–486–9005
Listening Library ..............................203–637–3616
Little Tikes ...................................800–321–0183
Living & Learning ..............................800–306–3013

Panasonic Interactive Media ....................888–726–2543
Pappa Geppeto's Toys .........................800–667–5407
Pastime Industries .............................800–488–5554
Patail Enterprises .............................800–990–0869
Patch Products ................................800–524–4263
Pearce-Evetts .................................800–842–9571
Peeleman-McLaughlin ..........................800–779–2205
Peerless Plastics .............................800–458–9595
PEP Publishing ................................800–842–9571
Perry Innovations ............................800–527–2966
PhotoPals of San Diego .......................800–765–7257
Planet Dexter/Addison Wesley Longman .......800–358–4566
Playmates Toys ...............................714–428–2000
Playmobil.....................................800–752–9662
PlaySkool ....................................800–752–9755
Play-Tech ....................................212–242–3020
Pleasant Company .............................800–845–0005
Pockets of Learning ..........................800–635–2994
Power Industries .............................800–395–5009
Pressman Toy Corporation .....................212–675–7910
Promotional Resource Specialty ................201–666–2100
Prospect Marketing Company ...................800–533–7618
Put-Together Developmental Toys ............315–637–2664
Quincrafts ...................................800–342–8458
Radio Flyer ..................................800–621–7613
Rainbow Village ..............................800–756–3012
Rand McNally .................................800–333–0136
Real Music for Kidz ..........................800–557–3262
Red Note Records .............................800–824–2980
Ritvik Toys ..................................800–465–6342
Rivertree Productions ........................800–554–1333
RMC ..........................................800–762–6443
Rock 'N Learn ................................800–348–8445
Rose Art Industries ..........................800–272–9667
Roylco .......................................800–362–8656
Safe-T-Child .................................800–828–0098
Sassy ........................................800–323–6336
SC&T International ...........................800–408–4084

Scholastic ........................................800–325–6149
Schylling Associates ...........................800–541–2929
Science Passports ..............................301–229–9630
Scientific Explorer ............................800–900–1182
Second Avenue Creations ......................800–713–1105
SEGA of America .............................800–872–7342
Set Enterprises .................................800–351–7765
7th Level .......................................800–884–8863
Shetland Toys ..................................415–358–3700
Sierra Club Books .............................415–977–5600
Skookum Jump Rope ..........................800–255–9526
Skools ..........................................800–545–4474
Small Fry Originals ...........................888–338–2444
Smartek Software ..............................800–858–9673
Snazaroo .......................................800–451–4040
Soleil Software ................................415–771–3940
Sony Wonder .................................800–221–8180
Soozaroo Music ...............................800–443–4727
Spizzirri Publishing ...........................800–322–9819
Sports Dynasty ................................800–656–4263
Spring Valley Creations .......................509–447–2907
Step 2 ..........................................800–347–8372
Steven Halpern's Music ........................800–909–0707
Steven Toys ...................................573–486–5494
Stewart Tabori & Chang .......................212–519–1200
Stoffle Enterprises .............................800–526–9569
StoryTime Creations ..........................800–557–8679
Straight Edge ..................................800–732–3628
Strombecker/Tootsietoy ........................800–944–8697
Sunburst .......................................800–786–3155
SunFeather Natural Soap Company ............315–265–3648
Sweet Pea/V-Link .............................800–830–5032
Table Toys ....................................800–999–8990
Ta-Dum Productions ...........................215–947–4751
T&M McCurry .................................707–895–2291
Talking Stone Press ...........................617–734–1416
Tasco Sales ....................................305–591–3670
TC Timber ....................................800–359–1233

Team Concepts ....................................800–486–0898
Tectron .........................................212–255–8388
Think A Ma Jig ..............................415–512–7930
3M ..............................................800–416–4061
TiffHill Productions ...........................888–462–5833
Tiger Electronics ..............................847–913–8100
TL Clark Educational Products ................800–566–1390
Today's Kids ...................................800–258–8697
Toddler Teepee ...............................888–377–2106
Toothaccount ..................................888–448–8376
Tootsietoy/Strombecker ........................800–944–8697
TopLine Toys ..................................800–347–4818
Toshiba America ..............................800–631–3811
Toy Biz .........................................800–270–4287
Toycrafter ......................................716–288–9000
Toymax .........................................800–358–8697
Toys for Special Children ......................800–832–8697
Toys to Grow On ............................800–542–8338
Toy Works .....................................518–692–9665
Trend Enterprises .............................800–328–0818
TS Denison ....................................800–328–3831
Twentieth Century Fox Home Entertainment ...800–800–2369
Twin Sisters Productions ........................800–248–8946
Tyco Toys ......................................800–488–8697
Uncle Goose Toys ............................888–774–2046
Uncle Milton Industries ........................800–869–7555
University Games ..............................800–347–4818
U.S. Games Systems ..........................800–544–2637
Video Tutor ....................................800–445–8334
Village Children's Production ..................800–287–2559
Voyagers .......................................800–767–3317
VTech ..........................................800–521–2010
Weeks Juvenile Products ......................800–400–8697
Westpier .......................................800–929–4125
What's Next Manufacturing ....................800–458–8635
Wild Goose ...................................800–373–1498
Wild Planet Toys .............................800–247–6570
Williamson Publishing .........................800–234–8791

STEVANNE AUERBACH, PH.D., is internationally known as Dr. Toy. She has been writing, speaking, and consulting about toys and children's products, child development, and parenting for more than twenty-five years. In 1987, she founded the world's first interactive toy museum, the San Francisco International Toy Museum at The Cannery, where thousands of children can view and play with toys from around the world. Dr. Toy's professional observations of children's play were fine-tuned during those years.

Dr. Auerbach has written many books and articles for parents and professionals. She has been a consultant and consumer spokesperson. She continuously evaluates and reports on toys and children's products for *Dr. Toy's Guide*, the award-winning magazine-format Web site on the Internet, and for her weekly syndicated column, "Dr. Toy," distributed by King Features Syndicate to fifteen hundred newspapers throughout the U.S. and Canada.

Dr. Auerbach, Director of the Institute for Childhood Resources, founded in 1975, worked for the federal government for many years in Washington, D.C. She evaluated educational Title One Programs, worked to improve national child-care services, established the first child-care center for the children of employees at the Department of Education, and approved the first grant for *Sesame Street*. Dr. Auerbach was the first educational consultant to the Living Stage Theatre Arts Program at Arena Stage. She has also been affiliated with the Far West Laboratory for Educational Research and Development, the Council for Exceptional Children, the American Counseling Association and other professional organizations. She is a longtime member of the National Association for the Education of Young Children, the American Specialty Toy Retailing Association, the American Association of Journalists and Authors, and Women in Toys.